THE CONTEMPORARY JESUS

THE CONTEMPORARY JESUS

Thomas J. J. Altizer

State University of New York Press

Published by
State University of New York Press, Albany

For information, address State University of New York Press
State University Plaza, Albany, NY 12246

Production by Dana Foote
Marketing by Theresa A. Swierzowski

Library of Congress Cataloging-in-Publication Data
Altizer, Thomas J. J.
    The contemporary Jesus / Thomas J. J. Altizer.
        p. cm.
    Includes bibliograpical references and index.
    ISBN 0-7914-3375-7 (alk. paper). — ISBN 0-7914-3376-5 (pbk.
alk. paper)
    1. Jesus Christ—History of doctrines. 2. Jesus Christ—History
of doctrines—20th century. 3. Jesus Christ—Influence. 4. Jesus
Christ—In literature.   I. Title.
BT198.A48   1997
232—dc21   96-39269
                                                             CIP

10 9 8 7 6 5 4 3 2 1

In Memory of
Albert Schweitzer

CONTENTS

Although there is an overwhelming interest in Jesus today, there is a deep gulf between our New Testament scholarship and our imaginative visions of Jesus, just as there is a comparable gulf between our biblical scholarship and our religious and theological understanding. Never before has biblical scholarship been so narrowly professional, or so fully isolated from the life of faith. One consequence of this is that we are being engulfed by a ravaging fundamentalism that is indifferent to critical scholarship, and understandably so, given the deep isolation of our most advanced and professional biblical scholarship. Only in the Roman Catholic world is genuine biblical scholarship truly engaged with the life of the church, and this might be the deepest source of the profound controversies that are now engulfing Catholicism. For true biblical scholarship inevitably challenges the Christian tradition, and does in its most ultimate grounds. Protestantism originated with this realization, but in our century Protestantism has been dominated by a new orthodoxy wholly isolating faith from a critical understanding of the Bible, as most deeply embodied in Karl Barth's *Church Dogmatics*. Here, a theology of the Word either dissolves or phenomenologically suspends all critical understanding of the actual words of the Bible. So now there is a chasm between theology and biblical scholarship in Protestantism, and one which is equally present in Catholic dogmatic theology. Indeed, theology is threatening to disappear in our time, and most so in the life of the academy.

Perhaps Marxism is alive today only in our academic world, although largely in the disguised form of "cultural studies," and Marxism is a profoundly secular theology whose continuing power is surely a mute witness to our inescapable longing for theology. In fact, we have been given remarkable Marxist studies of Jesus, and in liberation theology a Christian Marxism has been powerful in the church. If Marxism is truly ending in our world, we are once again confronted with a deep theological void that full modernity has known as the death of God. Yet the death of God was most profoundly envisioned and enacted by deeply Christian visionaries and thinkers, as witness Blake and Hegel. The first imaginative vision of the death of God occurs in Blake (in *America*, 1793), a Blake who is our most Christocentric visionary, and who imaginatively discovered a totally apocalyptic Jesus. This is the Jesus whom Hegel conceptually transformed into a pure and total dialectical negation, thereby transforming Christian apocalypticism into a purely logical and purely historical philosophical thinking. Even today Hegel remains our Aristotle, or our only truly systematic and comprehensive thinker. Yet Blake inaugurated an ultimately modern imaginative vision, creating our only truly modern imaginative "system," a system even more fully apocalyptic than Hegel's, and one grounded in a vision that is finally a vision of "Jesus alone" (the motto of his greatest work, *Jerusalem*).

Despite the fact that the apocalyptic Paul created Christian theology, apocalypticism is alien to virtually the whole world of theology, with the all too significant exception of Augustine's *City of God*, which has nevertheless been the most profoundly influential and germinal work in the history of Western Christian theology. The most unfinished and precarious work of Christian theology has always been eschatology. Significantly Barth was unable to complete his dogmatics with a projected fifth volume on eschatology, although eschatology is the deepest ground of primitive Christianity and of the New Testament itself. The dominant expressions of twentieth century theology have sought an ultimate dividing line between eschatology and apocalypticism, but it is now clear that such a division is finally impossible, so here we find yet another chasm between theology and New Testament scholarship. Our most profound imaginative visions of Jesus have always been, whether implicitly or explicitly, apocalyptic, as above all true in the modern world. Today our biblical scholarship and theology are alienated from the world of the imagination, and if only thereby alienated from apocalyptic vision itself. This book is an attempt to bring together the worlds of New Testament scholarship and imaginative vision, and inasmuch as it is the first such attempt, it will inevitably have grave limitations, not least because its author is not a New Testament scholar. Because New Testament scholars are silent on this crucial front, however, with the exception of my New Testament teacher, Amos N. Wilder, this chasm demands an attempted crossing. If this attempt fails, hopefully others will occur, otherwise we might as well confine New Testament scholarship to our museums.

This book is the culmination of many theological studies over a long period of time, beginning with an attempt to reach a Christian theological understanding of Buddhism. Buddhism has been essential to this quest throughout this voyage, and I remain grateful for my theological dialogues with Masao Abe and Keiji Nishitani, as well as for the assistance I have been given by American Buddhologists. My later work is most crucial to this study, most fundamentally my books: *The Self-Embodiment of God, History as Apocalypse, Genesis and Apocalypse,* and *The Genesis of God. Genesis and Apocalypse* and *The Genesis of God* incorporate my theological understanding of Hegel and Nietzsche, which is fundamental to this book, and the appendix to *The Genesis of God* cites most of the works that are important to my interpretation. Yet this book has been written in greater isolation than any of my previous books, with the exception of *The Self-Embodiment of God*, although it does renew a dialogue with my first theological partner, William Hamilton, whose most recent book, *A Quest for the Post-Historical Jesus* (New York: Continuum, 1994) is closer to this book than any other. I am grateful for John Dominic Crossan's spirited response to the chapter on his work, and I am grateful for the criticism I received from John B. Cobb, Jr. and Charles E. Winquist of an original and now abandoned first chapter. Yet it was Lissa McCullough's astute critical response which most sustained me while I was writing most of the book. Once again I am grateful to the State University of New York Press, particularly so to Dana Foote, the production editor of this book, and to Wendy Nelson, whose copyediting was truly challenging. The book is dedicated to Albert Schweitzer, the primal father of the apocalyptic interpretation of the New Testament, who has always been my one twentieth-century theological saint.

Nothing is a deeper mystery today than apocalypse, and this despite the fact that ours is so clearly an apocalyptic time, the deepest and most comprehensively apocalyptic time in our history. Jesus is certainly the inaugurator of what we have known as apocalypse, and yet Jesus is most unknown theologically as the inaugurator of apocalypse. So it is that the mystery of apocalypse is inseparable from the mystery of Jesus. We now know more about both apocalypticism and Jesus than we have ever known before, but paradoxically such knowledge is indistinguishable from the deep mystery of both Jesus and apocalypse. This is above all true theologically, for it is the Christian God whom we do not know as an apocalyptic God, or the God who is the deepest ground of apocalypse, and thereby the most ultimate ground of Jesus. Ironically, Barth himself, in his greatest theological work, could declare: "In Jesus, God becomes veritably a secret: he is made known as the unknown, speaking in eternal silence."[1] Certainly God is manifestly unknown to us in the apocalyptic Jesus, and equally unknown in the apocalypse that Jesus inaugurated, so the mystery of Jesus and the mystery of apocalypse may well ultimately be the mystery of God, a mystery that has never been so overwhelming as it is today.

Western, if not Eastern, Christianity primarily knows Jesus by way of the crucifixion. If the crucifixion is the beginning of the reversal of consciousness, as Hegel maintains, a reversal calling forth the depths of faith, then the death of Christ is for Hegel the touchstone by which faith itself is verified.[2] Yet Jesus' death is an apocalyptic death, and is so for Hegel, because it calls forth a totally new world and horizon. That is the world in which faith is "verified," and not in anything we can know as an ecclesiastical community or world. It was the very advent of what we have known as the Church which inaugurated the dissolution of apocalypticism. For even if most of the primitive Christian churches were apocalyptic communities, these disappeared or became heretical within the first three generations of Christian history. If this was the most rapid and most radical transformation of a new religious world that has ever occurred in the history of religions, no other historical tradition has so comprehensively transformed itself in the course of its history as has Christianity, just as no other tradition has generated such profound polarities between heresy and orthodoxy. So, too, no other tradition has engaged in such profound and violent conflicts over its own deepest center. Jesus is the center of Christianity, but a profoundly dichotomous center, generating not only deeply conflicting images and symbols of Jesus, but creating in the language, consciousness, and society of Christianity the most deeply dichotomous world in history.

Dichotomy itself could be a primal way of unveiling the mysteries both of Jesus and of apocalypse. Apocalypse is clearly dichotomous, for it is simultaneously the total ending of an old world and the total beginning of a new world, each inseparable from the other, and yet each the very opposite of the other. Therefore apocalypse is a *coincidentia oppositorum*, a full coming together of total opposites, the opposites of total ending and total beginning, and the opposites of a totally old world or aeon and a totally new aeon or world. Opposites in some sense are present throughout the history of religions, as witness what the historian of religions knows as the dichotomy between the sacred and the profane, or what the Buddhist knows as the dichotomy between nirvana and samsara, or what the Christian knows as the dichotomy between Christ and Satan, or sin and grace. Moreover, and as both Buddhism and Christianity make so fully manifest, the very depth and power of each opposite is inseparable from the power and the depth of the other. The totality of nirvana is inseparable from the totality of samsara, just as the totality of grace is inseparable from the totality of sin. Only by knowing the depth of nirvana can the Buddhist know the depth of samsara, just as only by knowing the depth of grace can the Christian know the depth of sin. Even if the Buddhist can know a liberation in which all opposition disappears, just as the Christian can envision a redemption in which sin and darkness disappear, such disappearance is the disappearance of an ultimate opposition, and apart from this opposition such a disappearance is wholly unreal.

The depth and comprehensiveness of apocalyptic faith are in virtually exact accordance with the immediacy and intensity of an apocalyptic expectation. So the apprehension of the immediate nearness, or even dawning, of the "end," calls forth the fullness of apocalyptic engagement, and equally and necessarily calls forth the radical negation of everything that stands forth and is given as "world." Here there is a deep and pure dichotomy, not only between old aeon and new aeon or old creation and new creation, but also between the very immediacy of an apocalyptic totality and the very reality of an old world. Full apocalyptic faith is an expectation of the "end of the world," an ending that will occur immediately, or is occurring even now. While nothing could be more absurd to the great majority of Christian believers today, there are few historians who do not now affirm that such an expectation was embodied in the greater body of primitive Christianity and even in Jesus himself. Nothing else has so profoundly alienated Jesus from our world, just as nothing else has been a greater challenge to twentieth-century Christian theology. But Christian theology has overwhelmingly been either antiapocalyptic or nonapocalyptic throughout its history. At no other point is there a greater unity among all the various and divergent forms of Christian "orthodoxy," just as in no other arena has Christian heresy been more deeply challenging to Christian orthodoxy, with the possible exception of the Arian challenge.

Arianism has been the most challenging Christian heresy throughout most of Christian history, an Arianism refusing the full and total deity of Christ by its affirmation of the full and total humanity of Jesus, a humanity apart from which there could be no real or actual crucifixion. Nothing has more deeply resisted theological understanding than the crucifixion, unless it is the apocalypse embodied in the crucifixion. This is just the issue through which orthodox theology has most deeply been disrupted, for this is the crucial point at which orthodox theology has been unable consistently and coherently to affirm both the full deity and the full humanity of Christ, and above all because it refuses the death of God in the crucifixion. Augustine's theological thinking is most ambivalent just at this point,[3] but such ambivalence disappears in Aquinas' fully systematic theological thinking.[4] There is a deep discord between Luther and Calvin in their understanding of the crucifixion, one seemingly reconciled in Barth's understanding of the crucifixion of Christ as the glorification of Christ.[5] Here, Barth is a unique theological thinker, and while he has thereby affected at least one major Catholic theologian,[6] it is precisely the theology of the cross that is most resisted by Christian theology as a whole. But it is most resisted by the refusal of Christian theology to be truly apocalyptic, and thus to understand the crucifixion as an absolute transformation of the deepest grounds of Godhead itself.

If this profoundly apocalyptic motif is alien to Christian theology, it is not alien to Christian imaginative vision, as is most openly manifest in the Christian epic tradition. Here, above all, we can know that a uniquely modern imagination is in deep continuity with earlier expressions of the Christian vision. Just as Dante is the deepest literary presence in Joyce's apocalyptic epics, Milton is the deepest literary presence in Blake's apocalyptic epics, even as *Paradise Lost* was profoundly shaped by the *Commedia*. The thesis could even be advanced that the apocalyptic Jesus is finally the only hero in our Christian epics. For even if the Christian epic hero or heroine is everyone, this epic everyone is finally the apocalyptic Jesus, and ultimately the crucified Jesus. Although Dante could seemingly know only the resurrected and heavenly Jesus, he nevertheless knew the incarnate body of Jesus in Beatrice, just as Joyce knew the apocalyptic and crucified Jesus in Here Comes Everybody and Anna Livia Plurabelle. The Christian epic voyage is a voyage into darkness and light at once, thus a voyage into Satan and Christ at once, either calling for or actually realizing a *coincidentia oppositorum* between Christ and Satan. New Testament scholars seemingly have very little interest in Satan, despite the fact that Satan or an ultimate darkness is more fully present in the New Testament than in any other scripture in the world. But Satan ever increasingly becomes the dominant presence in the Christian epic, until in *Finnegans Wake* Satan is all in all. Yet our epic Satan is inseparable from Christ. Even if he is the pure opposite of Christ in the *Inferno*, Satan and Christ are polar twins in *Paradise Lost*, and they comprehensively pass into each other in Blake's *Milton* and *Jerusalem*. So, too, the apocalyptic Jesus is inseparable from Satan, even as is the crucified Jesus, for in the depths of a uniquely Christian vision eternal life is inseparable from eternal death.

One of the most assured results of modern New Testament scholarship is a critical and historical deconstruction of virtually all our given and traditional understanding of the actual words of Jesus. Now we know that these words are most fully present in the parables of Jesus, parables deeply transformed by the synoptic gospels, which occurred not only by way of the grammatical and syntactical structure of their texts, but more deeply by a dissolution or dilution of the original assault of the parables. This assault can now be understood as enacting a radical negation of every given or established understanding of either God or the world. Although it is true that the parables renew an original prophetic assault upon all established faith and all established society, this now occurs in a finally apocalyptic situation, and all of the parables of Jesus are parables of the Kingdom of God. The dawning of the Kingdom of God draws forth these parables, and they are inseparable from Jesus' eschatological or apocalyptic proclamation of the Kingdom of God. So far as we can now know, it was Jesus alone who then employed the explicit title of *Kingdom of God*, just as it was only Jesus who taught primarily by way of parables. Moreover, his parabolic language is the most common language ever employed by a prophet or seer, being vastly distant from the biblical prophetic texts, and just as distant from the language of Christian theology. Finally, if not immediately, Jesus' parabolic language is the language of everybody or everyone. Nevertheless, this language reverses every given identity and assurance, most deeply reversing everything that is manifest or given as either

world or God. So that inevitably the parables were transformed in the memory of the primitive churches, and truly
reversed when they were later understood as mystical or
moral allegories.

Such a reversal of reversal has repeatedly been unveiled
as the very paradigm of all triumphant or established
Christianity. Perhaps it is most clearly and most fully
unveiled in the Christian epic, but also unveiled by our
deepest Christian prophets and seers, who again and again
have renewed a repetition of the apocalyptic and parabolic
Jesus. No doubt the purely common language of Jesus'
parables is one of shock and offense, and of the deepest
possible offense, so that it can only be heard by us as a
language of death, and even of eternal death. Yet eternal
death is here inseparable from eternal life, or ultimate
judgment inseparable from ultimate redemption, or the
kingdom of darkness inseparable from the kingdom of light.
Such an ultimate polarity and opposition is renewed
throughout Christian history, just as it is renewed in the
depths of a uniquely Christian consciousness, for Christianity embodies deeper internal conflict and discord than
any other historical tradition. If only at this fundamental
point, Jesus is surely the founder of Christianity. But he is
also the founder of what we can know only as an ultimate
revolution. Christianity reversed its founder more than did
any other historical tradition, but this could be a decisive
sign of an original revolutionary Jesus, whose way is so
revolutionary that it was inevitably reversed, and reversed
if only to make possible a Christian community and a
Christian world.

Kierkegaard, and every radical Christian, can know the
historical evolution of Christianity as a pure reversal of
original Christianity. Finally, this reversal culminates in
the end of Christendom and the death of God, but both

Blake and Hegel can know this ultimate death as a repetition of the crucifixion, and hence as both an historical and an essential realization of the original Jesus. Christianity has always known a contemporary Jesus as a repetition and renewal of the original Jesus, but if our dominant Christian traditions have truly reversed Jesus, then authentic renewals of Jesus will be ever more radical as Christian history evolves. This is just the movement we can discover in the evolution of the Christian imagination, or certainly in the Christian epic imagination. Dante, Milton, Blake, and Joyce were all theological revolutionaries in radically transforming the Christian world and vision that they inherited, and nowhere else may one discover such clear and manifest imaginative revolutions. Indeed, our Christian epics are more fully and comprehensively biblical than any other imaginative works, and, as opposed to all our dogmatic and systematic theologies, here the Bible is renewed as profoundly offensive, whose imaginative embodiment inevitably realizes an ultimate challenge to everything that is manifestly Christian. Not only are all of our great epic poets "heretics," but this is heresy that becomes ever more total as it evolves, and at no other point is there a deeper continuity between our epic poets. If only in our great epics we may truly discover a radical Christian tradition, and even if it is ignored by all our theologians and biblical scholars, here we may encounter an ultimate Christian challenge.

Yet our epic tradition is an apocalyptic tradition that becomes ever more fully apocalyptic as it evolves. The New Testament scholar can know apocalypticism only as an ancient or sectarian phenomenon, but in the Christian epic apocalypticism is simultaneously a new and a total vision, and it is total precisely to the extent that it is radically new. The radical Christian inevitably knows Jesus as the very embodiment of the ultimately and the absolutely new. Simply to be open to either the apocalyptic or the crucified Jesus is to be open to absolute novum, a new creation or a new aeon that is possible and real only as the consequence of the deepest ending. Now this is an ending that has continually been enacted in the deeper Christian imagination, and in the deepest Christian thinking too. But this enactment of ultimate ending is inseparable from a continual enactment of the truly and the absolutely new, for the repetition and renewal of apocalyptic ending calls forth ultimately new worlds. Hegel could philosophically know the eschatological or apocalyptic enactment embodied in Jesus, and above all in the crucified Jesus, as a pure and total negativity, a negativity that is the ultimate source of the forward movement of Spirit or Godhead and history at once. Similarly, Blake could envision the apocalyptic and crucified Jesus as the "Eternal Great Humanity Divine" that is the resurrection of a wholly fallen totality, a totality embodying deity, cosmos, and humanity simultaneously. The resurrection of that totality is inseparable from its eternal fall and eternal death, so that in Hegel and Blake alike, crucifixion and resurrection are finally and ultimately identical. If such an apocalypse is unique to Christianity, or to the deeper and purer expressions of Christianity, then so too is a fully and finally actual *coincidentia oppositorum.*

Only this *coincidentia oppositorum* embodies absolute novum. This is the novum that is the crucified and resurrected Jesus, a novum that can be and has been envisioned as an absolutely new and apocalyptic Godhead. That novum is inevitably a profound offense both to those who know God and to those who know the world, and if such an offense was first embodied in the eschatological proclamation and the parabolic enactment of Jesus, this is an offence that is ever renewed in the truly contemporary Jesus. This ultimate offense is present in the New Testament and the Christian imagination alike, at no other point is the latter more openly in continuity with the former, just as at no other point is the New Testament more fully alive in our history. Such an offense is a renewal and repetition of Jesus, but in being truly enacted as an offense it is a truly new offense, just as it embodies a truly contemporary Jesus. Thus the contemporary Jesus is a truly new Jesus, but precisely thereby a repetition of the original Jesus. This is the repetition that Kierkegaard could know as contemporaneity with Christ, and the Christ who is the absolute paradox of an absolutely self-emptied God.[7] If the crucified Jesus is ultimately the crucified God, God certainly becomes a mystery in Jesus, and an absolute mystery that Kierkegaard knew as the absolute paradox. But this mystery is deepened even if disguised in the evolution of Christianity, finally passing into the depths of darkness, a darkness Kierkegaard knew as the depths of God. This darkness, too, is present in the Christian imagination, and when embodied as an apocalyptic darkness it is not only inseparable from an apocalyptic light, but finally indistinguishable from that light. For the very advent of an apocalyptic totality is the advent of a totality that is all in all.

An ultimate *coincidentia oppositorum* can be apprehended as the deepest ground of a uniquely Christian apocalypse, one that is not only proclaimed and enacted by Jesus, but repeated and renewed in the deepest expressions of Christianity. Although ancient Christian orthodoxy wholly disguised or reversed this apocalypse, it is ever renewed in the deepest expressions of Christian heresy. Christianity is alone among the great world religions in not even evolving a full imaginative vision until after more than a millennium of historical evolution. Then imaginative vision is inevitably born as a heretical vision that becomes ever more fully and totally heretical as it truly evolves. Nowhere is this so clear and decisive as in the Christian epic tradition. Even Dante was condemned by the papacy as a heretic, Milton's one full theological treatise was so heretical that it could not even be published until two hundred years after it was written, and Blake and Joyce are so purely heretical that each effected a full and pure reversal of Christian orthodoxy. Yet a *coincidentia oppositorum* is at the very center of the Christian epic, as is a calling forth and voyage into an apocalyptic totality, and our epic totality is an apocalyptic totality if only because it embodies such a radical and total transformation. Here, this transformation is deepest in envisioning the depths of the Godhead itself, depths that are apocalyptic depths, and hence depths unveiling a new Godhead only by bringing an old Godhead to an end.

The simple truth is that Christianity, whether directly or indirectly, has always known Christ as an ultimate *coincidentia oppositorum*, a full coming together of time and eternity, of the finite and the infinite, of flesh and Spirit. Nothing else is a deeper offense in what the Christian most deeply knows as faith, yet a uniquely Christian *coincidentia oppositorum* historically evolves as does no other *coincidentia oppositorum*, with the possible exception of Buddhism. So that here and here alone, time and eternity, the finite and the infinite, flesh and Spirit, become progressively transformed in the Christian consciousness and world. While this does not occur by way of a manifestly continual evolution, it occurs nonetheless, as witness the deep differences between the primitive, the patristic, the medieval, the modern, and the contemporary Christian worlds. Christianity has known virtually innumerable forms of Jesus, and just as there are radically conflicting forms of Jesus in the New Testament, there are radically different forms and epiphanies of Jesus in Christian history. Not only are these commonly inconsistent with each other, but at bottom can be in opposition to each other, as is luminously clear in the early Blake's vision of Jesus in the *Songs of Innocence and Experience.* Unquestionably Christianity has called forth profound visions of Jesus, visions whose depth and power are unique, for while Buddhism has given us deep images of the Buddha, the deepest images of Jesus effect an ultimate shock or offense that is unique, as even an innocent Jesus is finally inseparable from the crucified Jesus.

Profound transformations have occurred throughout the history of Christianity, and no more total historical transformation has ever occurred than in the incredibly rapid transition from primitive to Catholic Christianity. The birth of Protestantism effected a comparable transformation, and the full advent of the modern world in the seventeenth century led to comprehensive transformations of Christianity in less than a century, culminating with the end of Christendom in full modernity. This is surely as momentous an historical event as has ever occurred in Christian history, comparable to the very birth of Christianity, for it inevitably poses the inescapable question of whether the end of Christendom is the end of Christianity itself. Yet the end of Christendom called forth as deep a Christian thinking as has ever occurred, as in Hegel and Kierkegaard, and it called forth truly new depths in the Christian imagination, as in Blake and Dostoyevsky. Modern secularization has been a deep de-Christianization, but it has no less been a deep re-Christianization. This, too, is a *coincidentia oppositorum,* and if the death of God is the symbolic center of a uniquely modern world, the crucifixion is the symbolic center of a uniquely Christian world. Each is an apocalyptic event, and not an apocalyptic event but *the* apocalyptic event, or that event which is the advent of a new world only insofar as it is the ending of an old world.

If the Christian apocalypse is finally a universal apocalypse, but one only gradually evolving in Christian history, is that apocalypse now everywhere, but truly nowhere in everything that is manifestly present? Apocalypticism has always known that the deepest darkness is fully realized only immediately prior to a total transformation. If the night of the world that we now know is just such a darkness, it too could be a decisive sign of a dawning apocalypse, a renewal even now of the apocalyptic Jesus. Certainly such a Jesus could only be invisible and unknown to us, and most unknown insofar as we are bound to past images of Jesus. Just as Jesus himself, in his eschatological proclamation and parabolic enactment, reversed every given form of God and the world, we must reverse every image of Jesus we have known if we are to be open to his contemporary and apocalyptic presence. Just such a reversal has continually occurred in the Christian imagination, a reversal not only of given images of Jesus, but also, and even thereby, a reversal of all given Christian images of God.

Ultimately apocalypse is the apocalypse of God. If ancient Christianity could reverse an original Christian apocalypse by knowing the absolute immutability and the absolute transcendence of God, a reversal of that transcendence and immutability is surely an apocalyptic reversal, one giving witness to, if not embodying, a new apocalypse of God. Certainly the Christian can know an apocalypse of God as having occurred in the crucifixion, for if the crucifixion is finally the crucifixion of God, it unquestionably embodies a truly and even absolutely new realization of the Godhead. This is the realization that is apocalypse

itself, and truly to know the crucified Jesus is finally to
know that apocalypse, an apocalypse that is ultimately
absolute actuality itself. Only that apocalypse is what the
Christian can ultimately know as either God or Godhead,
a Godhead that is all in all. That such a Godhead is most
invisible and most unknown today could be a genuine sign
of its very advent, an advent ending everything that we
have known as God. Thus an absolute transformation of
the Godhead, a transformation which is apocalypse, is simultaneously an apocalyptic ending and an apocalyptic
beginning. It is an apocalyptic ending of God, and thus
truly the death of God, and the apocalyptic beginning of an
absolutely new Godhead. Only the death of God could
make possible such a beginning, and if this occurs in the
crucifixion, and has been renewed again and again in the
deepest expressions of our consciousness and history, then
its renewal could be occurring again today.

Christianity has most deeply resisted Jesus by refusing
new epiphanies of the Godhead, this occurs at the very
beginning of Christian history, has occurred throughout
the history of Christianity, and is perhaps most deeply
occurring today. This can most clearly be seen in a refusal
of the crucifixion, one accompanied by exalted images of
the resurrected Christ of glory, a Christ who is wholly
removed from the crucifixion. Such a refusal of the crucified Jesus is certainly not confined to ancient Gnosticism,
it can be understood as the dominant Christian response
to Jesus, and one enshrined in a Christian orthodoxy refusing the death of God in the crucifixion. If the Christ of
glory is inseparable from an absolutely transcendent and
majestic Godhead, the apocalyptic and crucified Jesus is
inseparable from a kenotic or self-emptying Godhead. The
self-emptying God is the Godhead that is most ultimately
itself in crucifixion and apocalypse. This is the only

Godhead that could be present in the truly apocalyptic and truly crucified Jesus, a Jesus who is most distant from all Christian orthodoxies. But even as all orthodoxies and all churches are now in profound crisis, this, too, could be a sign of the renewal of the apocalyptic Jesus today. Yet the world itself is now in crisis, having lost everything that was once present as ultimate ground, a crisis that is manifestly an apocalyptic crisis, one threatening a final apocalyptic end.

Such an apocalyptic ending was first fully present in Jesus, and if such an ending is occurring even now, and occurring more universally historically than it has ever occurred before, Jesus could be fully our contemporary today, and more universally contemporary than he has ever previously been. Of course, this could occur only in the deepest darkness, a darkness that we assuredly know, and most fully know insofar as we are awake and alive. This darkness could be the site of a final reversal of the Godhead itself, a final reversal of every possible majesty and sovereignty of the Godhead, of every possible transcendence and glory. This is the very reversal that both Blake and Kierkegaard knew so deeply, one clearly a repetition and renewal of the original Jesus, and only thereby a truly contemporary Jesus. This is the contemporary Jesus who is the totally crucified Jesus, and therefore a kenotically apocalyptic Jesus, or that Jesus who is ultimately victim and servant, a servant and victim who is the very body of apocalyptic Godhead.

CHAPTER ONE

The Apocalyptic Jesus

Nothing has been more revolutionary in New Testament scholarship than the unveiling of the original historical Jesus as an apocalyptic prophet, and not only an apocalyptic prophet but one whose own words and acts were profoundly grounded in an ultimate and final apocalyptic enactment, an enactment even now of the advent or dawning presence of the Kingdom of God. We know that the New Testament title "Kingdom of God," with the exception of its occurrence in the Gospel of John (3:3–5), is an apocalyptic title, one wholly absent from the Hebrew Bible. It occurs rarely or never in all Jewish literature through the time of Jesus, even including the apocalyptic texts of the Dead Sea Scrolls.[1] At no point is the language of Jesus more clearly original than in its primary centering upon the Kingdom of God, and just as Jesus was the first prophet to proclaim and enact the actual advent or dawning of the Kingdom of God, that is an advent that here and here alone in biblical language is an ultimate and eschatological enactment. True, such an enactment is certainly present in the eschatological proclamation of Second Isaiah, a proclamation which is the very birth of Biblical apocalypticism, but neither here nor elsewhere in Jewish apocalypticism, with the possible exception of John the Baptist, is there an open enactment of the actual and final advent of apocalypse itself. Yet the language of apocalypse either perished or was deeply transformed in ancient Christian tradition, just as it was suppressed or wholly sublimated in medieval theological traditions, and even in the great body of Protestantism, so that the discovery of Jesus as an apocalyptic prophet came as a profound shock to the Christian world.

Now we know that the birth of apocalypticism gradually but decisively effected a profound transformation of Biblical traditions, and while we have little real knowledge of apocalypticism until the second century B.C.E., we can be assured that apocalypticism was as powerful as any other force in Israel. Although it assumed multiple and conflicting forms, it exercised a decisive role in Jewish rebellions against the new universal imperialism of the Hellenistic world. Ever since, apocalypticism has been a profoundly revolutionary force in Western history, perhaps our most purely revolutionary power. Just as apocalypticism played a decisive role in all of the great political revolutions of the modern world, from the English Revolution to the Russian Revolution and beyond, nothing has been more revolutionary in world history than apocalypticism, which not only made possible the original triumph of Islam, but also has been a fundamental ground of Marxism, and even of Asian Maoism. Moreover, it was Christianity that introduced apocalypticism into world history. Even if Hellenistic Christianity profoundly transformed the original apocalyptic ground of Christianity, it was Christianity that first actually embodied the universal horizon of apocalypticism, and if only thereby we can see that Jesus is the most revolutionary prophet in history. All too naturally, ancient and orthodox Christianity was impelled to disguise and transform the apocalyptic Jesus, a process that was already beginning in the earliest Christian tradition, and even in the New Testament itself, so that the historical discovery of the apocalyptic Jesus was truly a revolutionary event.

Nothing has been more alien to Christian theology than apocalypticism. Christian theology was created by Paul, as an apocalyptic theology, but apocalypticism very quickly moved to the periphery of the Pauline tradition itself, as it did in the Johannine tradition, so that by the second century of the Christian era apocalypticism virtually disappeared in a new Catholic Christianity. Thereafter it appears in Christian history only in deeply heretical expressions. Despite the dominance of the apocalyptic title "Kingdom of God" in the synoptic traditions, such a "Kingdom of God" has never truly entered Christian theology. Even today New Testament scholars commonly speak of the "Kingdom of God" as the "reign" or the "kingdom" of God, thereby repudiating the very possibility that Jesus broke away decisively from ancient Biblical traditions. But this break is already manifest in all genuine Jewish apocalypticism. The very possibility of eternal life is alien to all biblical traditions until the advent of apocalypticism. We know that apocalypticism, and this as early as Second Isaiah, could truly know God only by way of the advent of a total historical transformation. This transformation becomes a cosmic transformation in full apocalypticism, and hence a transformation truly and finally ending everything which we can know or name as "kingdom" or "reign." To insist upon knowing the "Kingdom of God" as the "kingdom" of God is surely to repudiate Jesus, or to refuse everything that is distinctively and originally his own.

Of course, ever since the discovery of the Dead Sea Scrolls virtually all historians know Jesus and early Christianity as arising out of the world of Jewish apocalypticism. But ever since the historical discovery of the apocalyptic Jesus, New Testament scholars and theologians have all too commonly engaged in the process of "de-eschatologizing" or "demythologizing" both Jesus and the New Testament, thereby clearly recognizing the subversive power of apocalypticism, and also thereby clearly renewing or repeating an ancient Christian transformation of Jesus. Even when such de-eschatologizing is seemingly anti-Christian, as in contemporary interpretations of the original Jesus as a Cynical Jesus, understanding the historical Jesus by way of a radical wisdom tradition, as present in the Gnostic Gospel of Thomas and a presumed early wisdom stratum of Q or the sayings source of the gospels of Matthew and Luke, such interpretation not only profoundly distances Jesus from his own deeply Jewish world and identity, but precisely thereby reveals itself as a deeply antihistorical interpretation. But flights from the apocalyptic Jesus are also thereby flights from the revolutionary Jesus, or flights from any kind of historical revolution, as so purely present in Christian Gnosticism itself. Gnosticism not only dissolves every possible humanity of Jesus, but also, and even thereby, dissolves every possibility of historical or even human transformation.

Inevitably, Christian fundamentalism, both Protestant and Catholic, is profoundly distant from the world of biblical scholarship. Indeed, modern fundamentalism came into existence as a rebellion against such scholarship, and even neoorthodox theology, which first arose in the second edition of Barth's commentary on Romans (1921), rebelled against the apocalyptic interpretation of the New Testament, and all neoorthodox theology, both Protestant and Catholic, has been deeply and consistently antiapocalyptic. This is most purely expressed in a Bultmannian demythologizing, which arose from Bultmann's critical acceptance of the apocalyptic identity of the historical Jesus, an acceptance demanding that an apocalyptic horizon be "demythologized," a de-mythologizing essential to the possibility of a contemporary expression of faith. Now we know that such demythologizing has occurred throughout the history of Christianity, and for Bultmann this fully begins with the Gospel of John, which he could interpret as being the most loyal of the four canonical gospels to the deepest "intention of Jesus." Nevertheless, for Bultmann, we can know nothing of the original person of Jesus, except insofar as we accept the Gospel of John and know that *"his word is identical with himself."*[2] Of course, that "word" is here a wholly demythologized word, one stripped of every possible mythical, cosmological, and metaphysical meaning. Only such a loss of every possible "objective" meaning makes possible the purely existential expression of faith. But just as apocalypticism wholly disappears in such a purely subjective faith, so likewise disappears every Word of God save that which is identical with Jesus himself, and in the end Jesus as the Revealer of God *"reveals nothing but that he is the Revealer."*[3]

While it is true that there are many forms of ancient apocalypticism, ranging all the way from a messianic expectation of a Messiah or sacred king to a fully apocalyptic expectation of the immediate coming of the end of the world, all of these are united in passionately opposing this world or this historical era or aeon, an opposition intending a full and actual inversion or reversal of the world, and such a reversal is the very essence of apocalypticism. As apocalypticism historically evolved, it moved ever more fully into an "other-worldly" direction, as manifest in the Qumran community or communities, and even more clearly manifest in a uniquely apocalyptic redeemer—that "Son of Man" whose coming will usher in the final judgment and the resurrection of the dead. Although it is now doubtful that Jesus identified himself as the Son of Man, or even spoke of the "Son of Man" at all, there can be little doubt that Jesus expected an immediate transfiguration of everything whatsoever, a transfiguration that even now is dawning. For the gospel, or "good news," of Jesus is the eschatological proclamation that the time is fulfilled, and the Kingdom of God is at hand (Mark 1:15). Nor can this proclamation be confused with the ancient Israelite belief that Yahweh or the Lord is the true "king" of the world, for Jesus not only proclaimed but enacted a total transformation of everything that is manifest or given as actuality or the world, a transformation which is the advent of the Kingdom of God.

The Kingdom of God for Jesus is certainly not a royal sovereignty, not an imperial nor even a messianic reign, but rather a full abolition or reversal of all given conditions. This is fully manifest in the authentic parables of Jesus, all of which are parables of the Kingdom of God. Nothing is more striking about the authentic words and acts of Jesus than their reversal of all human expectations whatsoever, and just as a methodological rule has been formulated to the effect that a gospel account of an act or saying of Jesus can be judged to be authentic to the degree that it embodies just such a reversal, the original Jesus has now been unveiled as a totally radical Jesus, and truly radical to the religious and social orthodoxies of his time and world. But no less so to our time and world, or to any historical or human world whatsoever, for the original Jesus is and was a revolutionary Jesus, even if not a revolutionary in the common sense. Nothing has been more problematic than our attempts to understand Jesus as a revolutionary figure, these have inevitably fallen short of understanding Jesus as a total revolutionary, except insofar as they have occurred in our deepest thinking and vision. The Jesus of Christian orthodoxy is surely not a revolutionary, or not as a truly human "son of man." But the Jesus of Christian heresy has commonly been a revolutionary, and the deeper the heresy, the deeper the apprehension of the revolutionary Jesus, and if a total Christian heresy has been realized only in full modernity, nowhere else is a vision of a revolutionary Jesus more fully or more totally at hand.

Christianity is unique in the history of religions in having undergone such a profound transformation in its very beginnings, and so much so that it is now impossible to apprehend any full or genuine continuity between primitive Christianity and Hellenistic and Catholic Christianity, even if such an orthodox Christianity is already at hand in the New Testament itself. At no point is there a greater chasm between radically different expressions of Christianity than there is between an apocalyptic and a nonapocalyptic Christianity. If we know that apocalyptic Christianity dominates the New Testament, by the second century of the Christian era, apocalyptic Christianity has become heretical, and all genuine apocalyptic expressions of Christianity have ever since been heretical. Often apocalyptic and orthodox forms of Christianity have warred within an individual figure or movement, as they did in Luther and early Protestantism, or in Milton and seventeenth-century Puritanism, thus effecting a fissure between the Magisterial and the Radical Reformation, and such fissures have occurred again and again in Christian history, and not least so in Catholicism itself. Apocalypticism has been most powerful, moreover, at the great turning points or crises of Christian history—as is true in primitive Christianity, in the later Middle Ages, in the early Reformation, in the deepest Christian movements of the seventeenth and nineteenth centuries, but most clearly so in the twentieth century itself.

Kierkegaard could know and realize an apocalyptic ending of Christendom, and do so in his revolutionary recovery or discovery of faith. So, too, Dostoyevsky could know or discover both Jesus and Christianity only by way of the apocalyptic ending of history. If Kierkegaard and Dostoyevsky are authentic prophets of our world, they are most clearly so as apocalyptic prophets, or prophets of the deepest ending. Certainly such prophetic judgments are not unique to the modern world. They have occurred again and again throughout Christian history, even as they have also occurred in Judaism and Islam. In the English Revolution they inaugurated modern political revolution, thence playing a decisive role in both the French and the Russian revolutions. In the twentieth century, however, apocalypticism has been universal as it has never been before, occurring not only throughout the world as a whole, but also decisively occurring throughout the whole spectrum of thinking, culture, and society, as Western history is truly manifest as coming to an end, a Western history that in full modernity became a universal history, so that the ending of Western history is thereby manifest as the ending of history itself. This was an ending which was already enacted in each of the great revolutionary thinkers and visionaries of the nineteenth century, including not only Kierkegaard and Newman, but also Blake, Hegel, Marx, and Nietzsche, each of whom were not only prophetic visionaries of our world, but apocalyptic enactors of a final and total ending, an ending which is nothing less than apocalypse itself.

How ironic that, in a world as apocalyptic as our own, theologians have been impelled to demythologize the apocalyptic ground of the New Testament, transforming the apocalyptic Jesus into a mysterious and humanly empty Word. Even if this is in full continuity with Christian theology throughout its history, only in the twentieth century has what the theologian knows as "myth" been so overwhelmingly real to humanity as a whole, and most real as an apocalyptic ending. Doubly ironic is the fact that Bultmannian demythologizing was fully created only in Nazi Germany, albeit by anti-Nazi theologians, and at the very time when the Holocaust was occuring, a holocaust which was surely an apocalyptic event. Even as Nazism itself was a profoundly pathological apocalyptic movement, occurring in the most deeply theological, if not the most deeply Christian, nation in the modern world. Certainly Nazism cannot be understood apart from apocalypticism, and just as Nazism is the most deeply negative or pathological apocalyptic movement that has ever occurred, it nonetheless enacted a truly apocalyptic ending, an ending which has even more comprehensively been enacted by twentieth century Communism, and with no less devastating results. The truth is, moreover, that a democratic and bourgeois world has realized a comparable ending, and while this has not been a violent and overtly catastrophic ending, it has nevertheless been a genuine ending. Not only is it the end or disruption of art, philosophy, and literature, but even more deeply the ending or abatement of our actual moral traditions, an ending inseparable from what we are realizing as the dissolution of a uniquely Western self-consciousness or a uniquely Western individuality.

It would be difficult if not impossible to name a truly major twentieth-century visionary or thinker who is not apocalyptic. Even twentieth-century theologians, who are overtly nonapocalyptic, and even antiapocalyptic, have nonetheless thought in the context of an apocalyptic ending, or at the very least in the context of the ending of Christendom. Our uniquely contemporary theology was generated by the ending of a Christian world, and employed as its conceptual ground the apocalyptic thinking of a Kierkegaard, a Nietzsche, or a Heidegger, each of whom

enacted the ending of our Western conceptual and historical traditions. Thus we face the fact that twentieth century
Christian theology has been apocalyptic and antiapocalyptic
at once, apocalyptic in its contemporary horizon and modern ground, but antiapocalyptic in its refusal of New Testament apocalypticism, despite the fact that the apocalyptic
Jesus is the original and primal ground of our apocalyptic
century and world. Only one New Testament scholar and
theologian has realized this primal truth, and that is Albert
Schweitzer, who not only gave us our purest and most
powerful apocalyptic interpretation of the New Testament,
but it was in this very context that he made his deepest
commitment to Jesus, a commitment that is unique among
our theologians. Accordingly, he can conclude *The Quest
of the Historical Jesus* with the affirmation that what is
eternal in the words of Jesus is due to the fact that Jesus'
words are grounded in an apocalyptic worldview, and con-
tain the expression of one for whom the contemporary
world with its historical and social circumstances no longer
had any existence: Jesus comes to us as one unknown,
without a name, he commands, and to those who obey
him, he will reveal himself in their labors conflicts, and
sufferings, and as an ineffable mystery, they shall learn in
their own experience "Who He is."[4]

Perhaps the deepest scandal posed by Schweitzer lies in
his understanding of Jesus' ethics as a truly revolutionary
ethics made possible only by the immediate advent of the
Kingdom of God. This advent will bring the world to an
end, so that Jesus' radical ethics could only be an interim
ethics, an ethics possible and real only in a truly apocalyptic situation. Thereby the radical commands of the Sermon on the Mount are occasioned and made real by that
brief interim between the present moment and the immediate coming of an apocalyptic Kingdom, a Kingdom whose

actual advent will bring the world to an end. But this ending releases the follower of Jesus from all obedience to the world, and only that freedom makes possible an actual following of Jesus. Schweitzer forcefully shows how Christianity lost this ethics, losing it already in the Gospel of John with its ground in a mystical regeneration, and then losing it also in the post-Pauline Hellenistic churches. All of this occurred because of the delay of the Parousia, the failure of the Kingdom of God to realize itself at once, and as that delay stretched into generations, Christianity abandoned its original apocalyptic ground. Consequently, it inevitably and necessarily abandoned the ethics of Jesus, transforming Jesus' revolutionary way into new ways making possible an accommodation to the world, and such de-eschatologizing of Jesus was deepened and expanded in virtually all of the subsequent expressions of Christianity.

Now it is true that apocalypticism poses a deep offense to all of us. But the deeper expressions of Christianity have always known the offense of faith, and thinkers such as Luther, Pascal, and Kierkegaard have even correlated the depth and truth of faith with the very degree and power of its ultimate and inevitable offense. Such offense has always been known by the Christian as being embodied in Jesus, and not only in Jesus as the full incarnation of God— the *coincidentia oppositorum* of time and eternity and of the finite and the infinite—but also in an all too human Jesus, who is nonetheless, and even thereby, the way, the truth, and the life. Why should it be inconceivable that "the way" is originally an apocalyptic way, one that has undergone profound transformations throughout its history, but also one which has returned again and again as an apocalyptic way, and most manifestly and universally so in our own time and world? What the theologian has failed to grasp is that apocalypticism is not simply an isolated and sectarian phenomenon, but rather an ultimate force and power that has realized itself in the fullness of our history, and in our most advanced and creative movements. How can one ignore the apocalyptic ground of Marxism? This ground is already and even more comprehensively and profoundly present in Hegelian dialectical thinking, and then bursts forth in Nietzsche, and after Nietzsche in the great body of our most ultimate and creative enactments. Apocalypticism is also a primal ground of the Christian epic tradition, as initially realized in Dante, and then expanded into ever more comprehensive apocalyptic expressions in Milton and Blake. This epic tradition becomes ever more fully and more finally apocalyptic as it evolves. Nothing could be clearer than the apocalypticism of Blake, who profoundly knew the apocalyptic Jesus long before this discovery occurred in New Testament scholarship. Blake renewed if he did not discover the purity of apocalyptic vision as a universal vision, and it is just as such that it is a breakthrough into truly new imaginative worlds.

Almost by necessity our theology is closed to such worlds. This is ironic, if such worlds are renewals and rebirths of the original apocalyptic Jesus, a Jesus whose enacted parables and eschatological proclamation called forth the very dawning of the Kingdom of God, a kingdom which can truly be known as an apocalyptic kingdom, and thereby as an absolutely new totality, a totality whose very dawning makes everything new. For an apocalyptic kingdom is a total kingdom, one whose realization brings an end to everything else, an ending which is itself an embodiment of the Kingdom of God, and an ending occuring so that God may be "all in all" (I Corinthians 15:28). Such an apocalyptic consummation is not only celebrated by both Jesus and Paul, it is at the very center of their primal words and acts, acts and words which simply cease to be themselves apart from such an apocalyptic ground. Apocalypticism is not simply an ancient phenomenon, or an isolated and sectarian world, for it has been renewed continually in ever more universal forms and expressions, until it becomes a truly universal world in late modernity. Everywhere apocalypticism has been grounded in an ultimate and final ending, and at no other point is there such a clear coincidence between our world and the world of Jesus. Even if Jesus proclaimed and enacted a Kingdom of God that is wholly opaque to us, ending as such is not opaque to us, an ending which he enacted as the triumph of the Kingdom of God.

Yet full modernity has known our apocalyptic ending as the death of God, an ultimate ending of our deepest ground, and therefore an ending that could only be an apocalyptic ending. It was precisely as such that it was celebrated and enacted by our deepest modern apocalyptic thinkers and seers. Although modern apocalypticism is certainly unique in centering its vision and enactment upon the death of God, it is not unique in enacting an ultimate ending, an ending that is a primal center of all apocalypticism. For just as apocalypticism can know a "new aeon" only by knowing an "old aeon" that even now is coming to an end, the depth and ultimacy of that ending is in precise accordance with the degree of totality of that "new aeon" that even now is at hand. So it is that an apocalyptic enactment of ending is thus ultimately and finally an ecstatic celebration of total joy. This is most clearly present in modernity in the total Yes-saying of Nietzsche and Blake, a Yes-saying that in some deep sense we know to be present in the beatitudes of Jesus. The beatitudes are an expression of his gospel or "good news," but they are meaningless apart from a total and final enactment. Nothing is more vacuous in New Testament scholarship than its exegesis of the beatitudes, at least when it knows them apart from an apocalyptic enactment, and just as both Blake and Nietzsche could know the gospel of the church as *dysangel* or "bad news," our nonapocalyptic understandings of Jesus have been wholly alien to the possibility of total joy, as most clearly manifest in a uniquely modern pietism and evangelicalism.

The death of God is the deepest event in modern apocalypticism, apart from which there is no possibility whatsoever of a truly new world. Is this an ultimate chasm between modern apocalypticism and ancient apocalypticism, or between our apocalypticism and the apocalyptic Jesus? Let it be confessed that Christianity has always known the death of God, and known it as occurring in the crucifixion of Jesus. Even if orthodox theology knows this death only as the death of the human Jesus, it is nevertheless an ultimate death and the sole source of redemption. Athanasius could defeat Arianism with his passionate argument that only the incarnation of a fully divine redeemer could be an actual source of our redemption, so that a Chalcedonian orthodoxy dogmatically proclaiming the true union of a fully divine and a fully human Christ is inevitably a witness to the death of God, even if this is not theologically realized until Luther. Nothing is more revealing about Christian history than the profound transformation Christianity underwent in its vision of the crucifixion. Images of the crucifixion do not truly enter Christian iconography until the end of the Patristic age. They are not a center of Christian art until the end of the Middle Ages, and poetic enactments of the Crucifixion do not fully occur until the seventeenth century. Nothing more clearly distinguishes Dante and Milton than the virtual absence of the Crucifixion from the *Commedia*, as opposed to its being the primal center of *Paradise Lost*. With

Blake, the Crucifixion is all in all, thus necessitating Blake's comprehensive enactment of the death of God, but a death of God is equally universal in Hegel's dialectical philosophy, which is certainly a crucial philosophical foundation of Nietzsche's proclamation of the death of God. If this ultimate and final event truly is an apocalyptic event, then it clearly has a Christian origin and ground, and one which Christianity at bottom has always known in knowing the ultimacy of the Crucifixion.

Christianity has undergone a profound transformation in its historical enactment, paralleled by no other religious tradition, with the all too significant exception of the transformation of pre-exilic Israel into post-exilic Judaism, which in its apocalyptic expression was the womb of Christianity. Profound transformation appears to be the very essence of Christianity: occurring not only in the first century of its history, but again and again throughout its history. In this perspective, a radical or even an apocalyptic transformation could be known as the very center of Christianity, and if Jesus is the true center of Christianity, an apocalyptic Jesus could be manifest as being that center, and even that center if he comes to us as one "unknown," and most deeply unknown in his very enactment of the Kingdom of God. Hegel could know an apocalyptic Kingdom of God as the totality of Absolute Spirit that enacts itself only by way of a pure and total self-negation or self-emptying, a kenotic self-emptying wherein Spirit realizes itself as the very opposite or "other" of itself, and does so through a logical and historical *Aufhebung* that is simultaneously the movements of negation, preservation, and transcendence. Hegel could know the depths of that *Aufhebung* as the Crucifixion or the death of God, a death that is the sole way to the absolute realization of Absolute Spirit, or to the final apocalyptic triumph of the Kingdom of God. Apocalypticism is reborn simultaneously in Blake and Hegel, but only through an apocalyptic, though now universal realization of the death of God. If Blake, and Hegel, and the whole world of modern apocalypticism, are deeply absent from modern theology, that may well be because even if only unconsciously modern theology knows all too deeply, that a contemporary apocalypticism could only be an enactment of the death of God.

Could it thereby be a repetition or renewal of the apocalyptic Jesus? Does an ultimate and final ending occur in the words and acts of Jesus, and an ending inseparable from a final realization of the Kingdom of God, an apocalyptic ending that is the true ending of everything which we can know and name as God? Such an ending is manifest for all to see in a uniquely modern apocalypticism, and is that a profound reason why we are so deeply closed to the apocalyptic enactment of Jesus, and so deeply alienated from an apocalyptic Kingdom of God? Nothing is more unique in Jesus than the centering of his acts and words upon the Kingdom of God, a Kingdom of God that is present and future simultaneously, or fully realized and vastly distant at once, or totally unveiled and totally mysterious simultaneously. Is such a Kingdom so purely opaque to us because we compulsively insist upon knowing it as the absolute sovereignty of a totally transcendent Godhead? Certainly that is a sovereignty, just as that is a Godhead that is wholly reversed in a uniquely modern apocalypticism. But if such a reversal is a rebirth of the apocalyptic Jesus, and a rebirth of his unique apocalyptic enactment that culminates in crucifixion, could that be the rebirth of a uniquely apocalyptic crucifixion, and a uniquely apocalyptic crucifixion that is finally a uniquely apocalyptic resurrection?

There may well be a far deeper continuity and even unity than we can imagine between an original Christian apocalypticism and a uniquely modern apocalypticism. Each is grounded in an ultimate and apocalyptic ending, just as each calls forth an absolutely new life and joy. And that apocalyptic joy or "resurrection" is inseparable from a final or apocalyptic ending or death, a death which is the death of God in modern apocalypticism, and a death that Blake could already know as an apocalyptic "Self Annihilation of God," a death embodying an absolute forgiveness of sin that is nothing less than a new creation, and a new creation which is an absolute love or compassion. Surely Paul knew such a compassion, and knew it as the consequence of the crucifixion and resurrection of Christ. And for Paul, as for the Fourth Gospel, crucifixion and resurrection are one event, just as they are for both Nietzsche and Blake, both of whom could know the death of God as the final advent of apocalypse itself. The death of God in modern apocalypticism is finally an absolutely redemptive event, just as the death of Christ is throughout the New Testament. But it is a death of cosmos or world in Christian apocalypticism, just as that death is the advent of an absolute chaos in modern apocalypticism, a chaos that is a uniquely modern nothingness or void. But both New Testament apocalypticism and modern apocalypticism can know that chaos as the consequence of an apocalyptic transfiguration. Each can know an apocalyptic ending as an apocalyptic transfiguration, and therefore finally know absolute death as absolute life. Now if that death is an apocalyptic death, and a totally apocalyptic death, it cannot be dissociated from the apocalyptic Jesus, a Jesus who was the first purely apocalyptic prophet, the one who first enacted a total apocalyptic ending—but an apocalyptic ending that is absolute beginning, a beginning that has been renewed again and again by those who embody him, or those who embody his acts and words.

CHAPTER TWO

The Jesus Seminar

While modern literary hermeneutics is an esoteric disci-
pline, our contemporary New Testament hermeneutics
would appear to be the very opposite, because it seeks a
common meaning of the New Testament, one that can be
understood by everyone whatsoever. Thereby Here Comes
Everybody is not only the reader or hearer of the New
Testament, but the author or authors as well, as most
forcefully embodied in *The Five Gospels: The Search for
the Authentic Words of Jesus*.[1] This is a collective report
on six years of work by the Fellows of the Jesus Seminar,
who are cochaired by two of the most distinguished New
Testament scholars in the world, Robert W. Funk and John
Dominic Crossan, and who comprise some seventy-five
American, British, and Canadian scholars, comprehending
secular, Protestant, Catholic, and Jewish perspectives. The
work of this seminar is not simply to attempt to recover
the original words and acts of Jesus, but to grade every
word of Jesus in the gospels in accordance with the prob-
ability of its having been said by Jesus, employing a
weighted average that is the numerical value assigned to
each saying by vote of the Fellows of the Jesus Seminar.
We are informed that this method was chosen because
that is the measure they use for determining grades in the
classrooms. So now our scholarly magisterium has given
us a graded gospel or gospels, the grades being reflected by

the colors red, pink, gray, and black. Red is employed for words that were most probably spoken by Jesus in a form close to the one preserved for us, bold black employed for inauthentic words that could not have been spoken by Jesus, and pink and gray as weak intermediaries between these two, and here less than 20 percent of the gospel words of Jesus are in red.

Immediately this volume unveils itself by its very dedication to Galileo Galilei, Thomas Jefferson, and David Friedrich Strauss, pioneers of our enlightened age, just as the philosophy of this scholarship is clearly a contemporary Enlightenment philosophy, as all miracle and mystery is dissolved. The editors do not hesitate to say (p. xvi) that these scholars have chosen to desacrilize the language of the New Testament, returning it to the common and secular language of the original gospels, thereby creating the first "scholar's version" of the gospels, one free of all ecclesiastical and religious control. Certainly the language of this translation is free of all religious or sacred intonation, as we are given a Jesus free of any possible Christian identity, and free of any imaginative or primordial power as well. Is this, then, truly a postmodern Jesus? While this Jesus is clearly intended to be for everyone, is this a Jesus who quite simply is everyman, or a Jesus who is Here Comes Everybody? Of course, the language of Jesus here is a universe removed from the language of *Finnegans Wake*, not only because it is literally prosaic, but also because it is a language which is simply impossible to imagine as the actual language of either voice or speech.

All too significantly, this Jesus is also removed from any possible historical ground, as the Jewish world of Jesus of Nazareth now becomes virtually invisible and unheard, except insofar as it is a world under assault. Once again Marcion is reborn, that second-century Marcion who created a Jesus wholly independent of any ground in the Old Testament. But Marcion was a deeply Pauline Christian, while this Marcionism is not only anti-Judaic but anti-Christian as well. Above all it is an apocalyptic world which here is banished, thus necessitating not only a radical isolation of Jesus from New Testament Christianity, but an equally radical isolation of Jesus from the only scripture that we have been given from Jesus' own historical world, the Dead Sea Scrolls. Although it would be impossible to exclude all apocalyptic language from a scholar's version of the language of Jesus, here an apocalyptic Kingdom of God becomes God's "imperial rule," and an apocalyptic Son of Man becomes a universal Son of Adam. Only one historical expression of religion in the ancient world is taken seriously here, and that is Gnosticism, so that not only is the Gnostic Gospel of Thomas here given full status as gospel, but it is accepted as the earliest written record of Jesus, or the earliest along with what is here presumed to be the oldest stratum of the Sayings Gospel Q (a hypothetical source of the gospels of Matthew and Luke).

Ancient and biblical history are excluded here as a matter of principle. Likewise excluded is the very possibility of an oral community or communities, with the declaration that oral memory truly or fully maintains only sayings and anecdotes that are short, provocative, memorable—and often repeated.[3] This excludes any possible historical veracity of the great bulk of the Old Testament, and also of the Homeric epics as well as Hindu, Buddhist, and Chinese scripture, as well as any possible historical memory for the great mass of humanity. It is as though contemporary humanity were the only humanity, and above all so the humanity of a new electronic age. Accordingly, scholarly thinking is simply identified with not only a nonhistorical thinking but a nonreflective thinking as well, which is the inevitable consequence of the adoption of an Enlightenment rationalism. Such rationalism is most manifest in its anti-Christian ground, and nothing is more continually repeated in this commentary than the insistence that the presence of Christian language in the gospels is decisive evidence of later fabrication, just as again and again it is reported that the Fellows rejected a particular saying because of its Christian overtones. Now even if there are overwhelming reasons to believe that the early churches transformed both the language and the person of Jesus, the Jesus Seminar would have us believe that it is not only an early ecclesiastical Christianity that negated the original Jesus, but quite simply Christianity itself. And once again Paul is presented as being the very opposite of the original Jesus, so that even a trace of Pauline language in the gospels is a crucial sign of distortion or fabrication.

So it is that the Christ of passion is wholly absent from this scholarly version of the gospels. Even the crucifixion itself is wholly marginalized, if not dissolved, and we are assured that we can know nothing whatsoever about it as a historical event. All that matters here are the sayings and the parables of Jesus, and even if there is little about them that is original, they are all that we here can know as the original Jesus. But something has happened on the way to this scholarly feast, for previously Crossan and Funk have given us extraordinarily powerful studies of the parables, revolutionizing our understanding of the parables in the past generation, unveiling the parables as effecting profound reversals of every possible expectation or understanding. Yet now both the language of the parables and the commentaries upon them reduce all meaning to the most common meaning, and all significance to the most commonplace significance. Even if we are informed that the original parables of Jesus induced both shock and offense, now that offense in the words of the commentary itself is shocking only in its modesty. Perhaps the best example of the minimizing of that offense is the acceptance of the Samaritan parable as a classic example of the provocative speech of Jesus the parabler. That parable might have been provocative to many of his hearers, but it would scarcely have been so to Galilean peasants, or to anyone today. Are we to believe that Jesus was most provocative in suggesting that one's neighbor could belong to a different ethnic group? The Cynics were far more radical, to say nothing of the prophets, so perhaps a real goal of this scholarly version of the gospels is to give us a Jesus who can neither shock nor offend.

At the very beginning of this volume we are given an absolute admonition, one printed in red to signify its absolute authority: "Beware of finding a Jesus entirely congenial to you" (p. 5). But it would appear that the Jesus discovered in the Jesus Seminar is wholly congenial to the Fellows of that seminar, or at least to the majority of those Fellows. Indeed, the work of this seminar has largely succeeded in erasing or dissolving any real originality of Jesus, a difficult feat given the absence here of a historical perspective. This most clearly occurs in the commentary on the Sermon on the Mount, where we are informed that the so-called golden rule is a piece of common lore found in ancient sources, Christian, Judean, and pagan, and that in its traditional form the golden rule expresses nothing that cuts against the common grain, or surprises and shocks (p. 156). Nothing is cited here that truly parallels or even fully suggests the golden rule, but that is presumably unnecessary if all enlightened people know that Jesus was unoriginal. Indeed, the only words printed in red in this version of the Sermon on the Mount are: "Our Father."

How significant, since there is virtually no theological analysis in the commentary, no attention given to what Jesus might have meant in addressing or speaking of God. It is almost as though Jesus didn't speak of God at all. Now it is true that few New Testament scholars now speak of God, or few if any in elite circles, and one could read this report of the Jesus Seminar without even being aware that there is a theological or religious ground in the original words of Jesus. Is that the revolutionary achievement of the Jesus Seminar? Was Jesus at bottom wholly without any sense of the presence or reality of God?

A primary text in virtually all critical theological analysis of the gospels is Mark 1:14, which records the inauguration of Jesus' ministry, and which just a short time ago was commonly accepted as being as close as we can come to the original Jesus. In the Scholar's Version, these words are all printed in black, signifying that they are wholly inauthentic:

> The time is up: God's imperial rule is closing in. Change your ways, and put your trust in the good news!

Now even if these words could not be the words of Jesus, the Fellows of the Jesus Seminar are convinced that Jesus did speak of "God's imperial rule," since that language so dominates the sayings and parables at different levels and stages of the Jesus tradition. But the majority of the Fellows do not believe that this is apocalyptic language, for Jesus did not and could not have proclaimed the end of history, if only because this is alien to the authentic parables and aphorisms. Why? Because in the judgment of the Seminar, Jesus spoke most characteristically of God's rule as close or already present but unrecognized, and thus in a way that challenged both apocalyptic and nationalistic expectations (p. 40).

Wholly absent here is any recognition of what until only yesterday was the dominant judgment of New Testament scholarship, namely, that the Kingdom for Jesus was both present and future, both already at hand and yet only to be consummated in the near future. Clearly, the Fellows have simple accepted or returned to C. H. Dodds's *The Parables of the Kingdom*, published in 1933, which maintained that in the parables the Kingdom is wholly present, thence coining the phrase "realized eschatology." But in the same year, Rudolf Otto gave us *The Kingdom of God and the Son of Man*, still the finest analysis of the Kingdom of God in the New Testament from the perspective of the history of religions, and Otto employed the image of "dawning" to draw forth the temporal significance of the Kingdom of God for Jesus.[2] This is the understanding that became the primary critical understanding, so that it is only yesterday that realized eschatology has been reborn, and then only under the impact of our new understanding of Gnosticism. Yet realized eschatology is not fully present in the Jesus Seminar, which can also judge that the Kingdom for Jesus was both present and future, even if it seemingly has no awareness that this is the dominant contemporary understanding of Jesus' language as an apocalyptic language.

One almost has the sense that the Fellows of the Jesus Seminar have little awareness of any world outside their own, and certainly little theological awareness, except to realize how opposed they are to all historical Christianity. But why such intense interest in an original Jesus? If this has no theological dimension, and little critical ethical emphasis as well, is it sustained by a deep embodiment of our contemporary world? And is that world a truly atheological world? At this point the Jesus Seminar may well be of deep theological significance, and the most profound change in biblical scholarship in the past two generations has been the diminution of all apparent theological interest. Who could believe that it would be possible to devote so much work to a quest for the original Jesus in the absence of all real theological perspective? True, this largely occurred in the Enlightenment, just as it was a major factor in the nineteenth-century quest for the historical Jesus, and a decisive ground for liberal Protestantism as a whole. All of these movements were most deeply German movements, and they were reflected in modern German philosophy, and above all so in two of the greatest modern German philosophers, Hegel and Nietzsche.

Hegel wrote his essay on the life of Jesus in 1795 when he was twenty-five and very much under the impact of the French Revolution.[3] While this essay was most shaped by the Gospel of John, Hegel's most beloved gospel throughout his life, nonetheless it is a truly philosophical essay, and perhaps nowhere else does a philosophical Jesus more fully coincide with a historical Jesus. One has only to read this essay to realize how vapid are all the theoretical judgments in *The Five Gospels*, and how a truly critical portrait of Jesus is inevitably a radical and challenging vision that challenges all given and established thinking. Nor can we forget that Hegel was the graduate of a theological seminary who had absorbed much of the New Testament scholarship of his time, and that was a time when biblical scholarship inevitably posed deep risks that are unknown today. Now it is true that Hegel had not yet made the deep breakthrough to his own unique thinking, but now that we know that a uniquely Hegelian thinking is a profoundly theological thinking, centered in what the Christian knows as creation, incarnation, crucifixion, and resurrection, we

can see how Hegel's early wrestling with Jesus was fundamental to that subsequent breakthrough.

Hegel, too, repudiates both a messianic and an apocalyptic Jesus, but the center of this essay is the way of the
cross, a crucifixion that is the inevitable consequence of
the absolute autonomy that Hegel's Jesus both teaches and
embodies. So that a crucifixion that is so peripheral to the
Jesus Seminar is primary to the young Hegel, and even
more deeply primal to the mature Hegel, who was the first
thinker to think the death of God. Indeed, it was precisely
by realizing true modernity as a modern realization of the
death of God, a realization which is the consummation of
world history, that Hegel could realize the ultimate and
absolute importance of the original Jesus. Not only does
The Phenomenology of Spirit culminate with the crucifixion, "the Calvary of Absolute Spirit," but a repetition of
crucifixion occurs in every deep actualization of what Hegel
knew as consciousness and self-consciousness, just as crucifixion and resurrection are the symbolic core of a uniquely
Hegelian dialectical negation or *Aufhebung*. So it is all too
clear why Jesus was absolutely fundamental to Hegel, and
just as he insists that his understanding of Spirit is inspired by the understanding of Spirit or the Paraclete in
the Fourth Gospel, the gospels themselves, are continually
reenacted in Hegel's thinking, and above all so that passion story which so dominates the original gospels.

In the Scholar's Version of the gospels, all of the words
of Jesus in the passion story are printed in black, signifying
that the historical Jesus could not possibly have said them,
save for the prophecy of the destruction and resurrection
of the Temple. So likewise are printed in black all of Jesus'
prophecies of his death or crucifixion. Nothing is allowed
to stand here that could be a possible ground for faith in
the Crucified Christ, nor for that matter for faith in the

Resurrected Christ. Above all it is any classical or traditional or even historical form of Christianity which is challenged here, or at least it could have no possible positive relationship to the original Jesus. Yet all too ironically this translation and commentary simply assumes that any form of New Testament Christianity itself could only be an orthodox Christianity. Accordingly, Jesus could not have been an apocalyptic prophet because most New Testament Christianity is apocalyptic, despite the fact that primitive Christian apocalypticism was so profoundly transformed and reversed by the advent and then triumph of an orthodox and Catholic Christianity. The truth is that *The Five Gospels* is a profound apology for orthodox Christianity, and is so if only because it establishes such an overwhelming gulf between the original Jesus and the great body of the New Testament, including, most certainly, the four canonical gospels. Thereby it fully sustains the claim of orthodox Christianity to be New Testament Christianity, and faced with a responsible choice between the Jesus of the Jesus Seminar and the Jesus of orthodox Christianity, how could one possibly oppose orthodox Christianity?

But it is possible to imagine Nietzsche's response to the "Scholar's Version" of the gospels, and we have it in the late Nietzsche's violent assault upon David Friedrich Strauss, for Nietzsche was far more contemptuous of the liberal Jesus than of the orthodox Jesus, a liberal Jesus which is the very incarnation of a uniquely modern decadence. While Nietzsche's *The Antichrist* is almost wholly unknown to New Testament scholars, it is nevertheless perhaps the most original and certainly the most radical unveiling of the historical Jesus, and also the one that establishes the greatest possible distance between Jesus and orthodox Christianity. *The Antichrist* is, indeed, a deeply and profoundly theological work, and not only is it

Nietzsche's last completed book, but it was written as the first volume of what was to have been his ultimate work, *Revaluation of All Values*. And the Jesus of *The Antichrist* is not only the very opposite of the Christ of the Christian Church, but is both the forerunner of Nietzsche's Zarathustra and the only historical figure Nietzsche knew who was free of all *ressentiment*. Nietzsche understands the proclamation of Jesus as the abolition of all sin and guilt: any distance between man and God is now abolished, and grace or blessedness is now the *only* reality. That reality is now lived in an absolutely new praxis, and even if Jesus is the only Christian, his life and death were nothing other than this praxis, a praxis dissolving all *ressentiment*, thereby releasing a truly universal love or acceptance. *Jesus* for Nietzsche is the name of the total forgiveness of sin, but a total forgiveness of sin which is inevitably and necessarily the abolition of that Christian God whom Nietzsche now unveils as the deification of nothingness or the will to nothingness pronounced holy (*The Antichrist* 18). This is that unique forgiveness which ecstatically is the dance of Eternal Recurrence, a forgiveness which is finally an absolute Yes-saying, a Yes-saying not only made possible by but actually embodied in Jesus.

If only from the perspective of Hegel and Nietzsche we can see how profoundly nonhistorical the Jesus of the Jesus Seminar is, and if that Seminar is wholly indifferent to the question of the relation between Jesus and God, and proceeds as though the question of God is of no real significance at all in the language of Jesus, it is difficult to imagine how it would be possible to create a more nonhistorical Jesus. It is as though Jesus had no actual relation to the whole horizon of the Bible, no relation other than a negative relation to a prophetic and apocalyptic Israel, and no relation other than a purely negative relation between Jesus and God. How else account for the translation of *basileia tou theou* as "imperial rule of God?" This translation not only associates Jesus' God with the oppressive rule of the Roman Empire, but wholly distances Jesus' God from any possible Old Testament ground. The only historical tradition that is allowed to be associated here with the historical Jesus is an ancient wisdom tradition, one that virtually dissolved everything the prophetic and the legal traditions of Israel know as God, but that this commentary sees as being renewed in the Gospel of Thomas. Now given the conviction of most of the Fellows that the great majority of the acceptable sayings and parables of Jesus are derived from Thomas and the presumed earliest stratum of Q (which for these scholars is free of all apocalyptic language), this almost means that only wisdom parables and sayings are acceptable, despite the fact that this reduces them to a very prosaic level of meaning indeed. So it is that Thomas has preserved what the Fellows take to be the form of the parable of the sower that is closest to the original, but here is a very ordinary story with neither reversal nor shock, even if it is the most natural or rational story. Is that what a parable of Jesus parables really is?

Why such deep respect for the Gospel of Thomas alone? True, the Fellows share a comparable respect for a hypothetical primitive Q stratum stripped not only of all apocalyptic overtones but also of all hint of the crucifixion. No doubt Thomas and Q are also deeply attractive to the Fellows because they are free of the passion story, just as they are free of all narrative form or structure. Is this the earliest written Jesus tradition, the one closest to the historical Jesus? Note the absence here both of an apocalyptic Kingdom and of a passion or crucifixion. What the Enlightenment most scorned is now surgically removed from the original Jesus, a surgery presenting itself as being scholarly reconstruction. And what is left? A purely primordial Jesus, or a Jesus who is the embodiment of a primordial wisdom, a wisdom truly alien to the Jewish world of Jesus, but that decisively appears in the Gnostic Gospel of Thomas? There is a little noted chasm among New Testament scholars today, one deriving from a division between those who are most affected by Jewish apocalyptic literature, and above all so by the Dead Sea Scrolls, and those who are most affected by the ancient Gnostic library discovered at Nag Hammadi, a Coptic library including the Gospel of Thomas. How significant that there are virtually no references to the Dead Sea Scrolls in *The Five Gospels* and a deep centering upon the Gospel of Thomas. So likewise the prophetic tradition of Israel is also largely ignored, no doubt because it is a deep influence upon the canonical gospels while being invisible not only in Thomas but in the Nag Hammadi scriptures as a whole. Are we to believe that we can recover the historical Jesus only through ancient Christian Gnosticism?

Unfortunately, no religious world is more deeply mythical than the world of Christian Gnosticism. A genuine Enlightenment critic would respond to the Nag Hammadi scriptures with an orgy of assault, which makes one wonder about the professed enlightenment of these scholars. Could it be a Gnostic enlightenment? One pruned, of course, of ancient mythical language, but one nevertheless aligned with the Gnostic language of the Gospel of Thomas? The commentary concedes that this is an incipiently Gnostic language, and certainly the Jesus of Thomas is a Gnostic redeemer, who has descended to earth and ascended to heaven, reminding the chosen ones of their ultimate origin in heaven, and being himself not only a model of, but the way to, an ultimate return to heaven. This is a Jesus who is not only far more ascetic than John the Baptist, but also absolutely indifferent to every actuality of the world as world. It is simply impossible to imagine a more otherworldly Jesus, a Jesus who is a heavenly Jesus alone, and who is wholly free of every possible historical tradition or world. Is such a Jesus a truly postmodern Jesus? An absolutely ahistorical Jesus but precisely thereby a primordial or ultimate Jesus?

CHAPTER THREE

Crossan's Jesus

There is one member of the Jesus Seminar whom it is very difficult to associate with most of the judgments in *The Five Gospels,* and that is its cochairman, John Dominic Crossan. Crossan has given us what is commonly regarded as the most important book on the historical Jesus published in our time, *The Historical Jesus,*[1] just as he has been both our most creative New Testament scholar since Bultmann and the one who has most fully absorbed contemporary literary criticism and theory. But Crossan's book on Jesus is a truly historical study, even if its methodology is unique, revolving about a triple triadic process: "The first triad involves the reciprocal interplay of a macrocosmic level using cross-cultural and cross-temporal social *anthropology,* a mesocosmic level using Hellenistic or Greco-Roman *history,* and a microcosmic level using the *literature* of specific sayings and doings, stories and anecdotes, confessions and interpretations concerning Jesus" (p. xxviii). Crossan insists that all three levels—anthropological, historical, and literary—must cooperate fully and equally, so that a methodological triadic equality is a fundamental goal of the volume.

Indeed, in responding to friendly critics at a recent conference on this book, Crossan confessed that he intended to be a new Schweitzer, initiating the third quest for the historical Jesus, the first being the nineteenth-century quest that culminated with its reversal in Schweitzer, the second being the Bultmannian and new hermeneutical quest that fully ends only with Crossan.[2] Crossan can also identify himself as a "Catholic with the soul of a leprechaun."[3] A leprechaun, it is to be remembered, is an elf in Irish folklore who can reveal hidden treasure if caught. The challenge, of course, is to catch this leprechaun, who is perhaps disguised even to himself, and surely uncatchable by any of our theological nets. Nevertheless, the word *Catholic* here is not to be ignored, and if the center of the book is its thirteenth chapter on "Magic and Meal," this is a deeply Catholic center, even if it is wholly distant from all hierarchical or even ecclesiastical Catholicism.

Crossan's Jesus is not only a Mediterranean Jewish peasant, but a Jewish Cynic and magician, and both Cynic and magician for Crossan are enactors of an eschatological world-negation, a negation of all established society and religion. Now Jesus is established within a peasant world in turmoil, one soon leading to a peasant revolt, which Crossan sees as a fundamental ground of the Jewish-Roman War of 66–70 C.E., an eschatological war ushering in the end of both primitive Christianity and the Judaism of Jesus' time. Yet Crossan's Jesus is not wholly bound to his own time, for in being the reverser of all established hierarchy, his is a call to the unclean, the degraded, and the expendable, for these are the "poor" who are blessed by the advent of the Kingdom of God. Such a Kingdom is a "kingdom of nobodies," a Kingdom not only under a divine rule transcending all human rules, but a Kingdom reversing every human judgment and law, and this even in the most literal and brutal sense. Crossan leaves no room for doubt that the Romans would have had every reason to execute Jesus, and not only the Romans but the Jewish social and religious hierarchy as well, for this is truly a revolutionary Jesus, even if he is innocent of any political program. Crossan does not assert that Jesus actually initiated a peasant revolt. But he makes it all too clear that if Jesus did have an initial historical impact, it could only have been in such a revolt. Such a revolt did, indeed, occur, and even occurred as an apocalyptic rebellion, a rebellion ending an old world and seeking an absolutely new world.

Unlike the majority of his compeers in the Jesus Seminar, Crossan has an acute apocalyptic sensibility, even if he can identify Jesus as antiapocalyptic, and seek to unravel Jesus' Kingdom as an antiapocalyptic Kingdom. But this is so only insofar as *apocalyptic* refers wholly to a future reality. Nothing is firmer in Crossan's judgment than that the Kingdom for Jesus is wholly a present Kingdom, and not only a present Kingdom but an enacted Kingdom, an enactment that is the very center of Jesus' words and acts. Accordingly, even Jesus the magician is an enactor of the Kingdom of God, for the exorcisms and healings are "what the Kingdom looked like at the level of political reality."[4] Apart from these magical exorcisms and healings, Jesus' Kingdom would be but an ecstatic dream without immediate social repercussions, social repercussions calling in the Kingdom here and now. This Kingdom invites outcasts above all, as in the parable of the wedding feast, and the social challenge of an "egalitarian commensality" is the radical threat of the parable's vision; commensality is the very center of the original Christian community, which was inaugurated by Jesus himself.

This is a crucial point at which Crossan's deep Catholic roots are manifest, for not only does he refuse to admit any dichotomy between the historical Jesus and the Catholic Christ, but he sees Jesus himself as the inaugurator of an egalitarian commensality that the radical Catholic knows as the Church or the Body of Christ. And this is truly a corporate body, one centered in an actual meal, a meal which is not only an egalitarian meal, but an ultimate meal as well. We are what we eat Crossan assures us, but true eating is above all a social act, and here a social act embodying a social revolution. That is the social revolution that is the advent of the Kingdom of God. Even if it has been reversed again and again, and above all reversed by an imperial and hierarchical Catholic Church, it nevertheless is a universal or catholic revolution, and even a resurrection that never happened but always happens. Crossan is also Catholic in his antiapocalyptic stand, for Catholicism came into existence as a transformation of a primitive Christian apocalypticism, an immediate and comprehensive transformation far greater than any other in the history of religions. At no other point is Crossan closer to St. Augustine, whose *City of God* is the deepest theological ground of Roman Catholicism, for while Augustine here rarely identifies the City of God with the Catholic Church, he is capable of asserting that the Church even now is the Kingdom of God and Kingdom of Heaven (XX, 9).

Nevertheless, Crossan is deeply ambivalent about apocalypticism, for even though he chooses to view Jesus primarily by way of a wisdom or sapiential tradition, he acknowledges that sapiential and apocalyptic understandings of Jesus were both well developed and simultaneously present at a very early stage of the Jesus tradition, and that these twin interpretations seem equiprimordial visions of Jesus (p. 230). Here, he is clearly distancing himself from the majority of the Fellows of the Jesus Seminar. The Fellows and Crossan would appear to agree that Jesus accepted apocalypticism in being baptized by John the Baptist and opposed it in moving away from the Baptist, but

Crossan's Jesus is just as fully an apocalyptic enactor as he is a wisdom enactor, and is so if only because he is the enactor of a truly new world. Of all the texts in the early Jesus tradition, the Gospel of Thomas is most deeply and purely antiapocalyptic, a gospel seeking a return to a primordial unity that is inseparable from a radical and total cosmic abandonment (p. 267). Crossan refuses to accept Thomas's Jesus as an historical portrayal of Jesus, and just as the Gospel of Thomas is a genuine seed of a fully developed second-century Gnosticism, this is clealry a trajectory that is a profound if not total transformation of the original Jesus. Indeed, Crossan has recently asserted that he imagines early Christianity developing with three major wings: to the right, a conservative Legal Christianity; to the left, a radical Gnostic Christianity; and in the center, a Catholic or Universal Christianity.[5] And there can be no doubt where Crossan himself stands!

Nothing in Crossan's book on Jesus is more astute or more engaging than his historical deconstruction of Josephus, particularly his criticism of Josephus's calling forth a "fourth philosophy" or ideology of Judas the Galilean, which Josephus sees as the single root cause of the devastating and revolutionary events of the next sixty years (6 C.E. to 66 C.E.). Josephus's fourth school of philosophy is quite simply apocalypticism, and even if it is a construct of Josephus's conservative imagination, it would be difficult to deny the enormous power of apocalypticism in this period of Palestinian history. While this may well be a peasant apocalypticism, as Crossan believes, it is just thereby socially and politically revolutionary, but no more revolutionary than subsequent apocalyptic movements. Genuine apocalypticism is inevitably revolutionary, and is so even when it is seemingly nonpolitical. Accordingly, Crossan refuses to identify Jesus as a Zealot or a peasant urban bandit, one wholly given to a political, apocalyptic rebellion, but nevertheless understands the historical Jesus as a profoundly revolutionary figure. Moreover, for Crossan, Jesus the Galilean is far more revolutionary than was Judas the Galilean, and not simply because of his enormous impact upon subsequent history, but also because his was a revolutionary way that was fully incarnate, and incarnate in the full actuality of life and world itself.

Crossan's book on the historical Jesus is truly remarkable, if not unique, not only because of its triadic methodology but also because it so fully fuses the acts and words of Jesus, as Jesus ceases to be that Jesus who is Word and Word alone, as in the dominant expressions of Protestant theology, and is called forth as that Jesus who is wholly an embodied Jesus: "In the end, as in the beginning, now as then, there is only the performance" (p. xxvi). While that performance is genuinely revolutionary, being wholly inseparable from an actual social revolution, it is also a fully incarnate performance, one actually embodied in "magic" and "meal." All too significantly Crossan can employ only the most radical language in speaking about what the Catholic knows as the Church, a radical language deconstructing two thousand years of ecclesiastical tradition, for only thereby can an original Jesus be manifest and actual once again. Could this nevertheless be a profoundly and uniquely Catholic deconstruction? If ours is a time in which Catholic biblical scholarship is first becoming fully comprehensive and truly real, is that a scholarship which is not only deeply challenging Protestant hermeneutics, and a traditional Catholic dogmatics as well, but also one that is calling forth a truly new but nevertheless primordial Catholicism?

One cannot fail to observe how deep the primordial motif is in Crossan, one which is surely a ground for his deep engagement with the Gospel of Thomas, but which is far more deeply present in his intended union of Kingdom and Wisdom. Nothing is more truly original here, for even if it is grounded in von Rad's unveiling of the wisdom tradition as an original ground of prophetic eschatology, here the focus is wholly upon the Kingdom of God in the Jesus tradition, a Kingdom that Crossan would unveil as a sapiential Kingdom. That is just why Crossan is antiapocalyptic, but this is the refusal of a nonsapiential or a non-primordial Kingdom, a Kingdom that is wholly and only future, and only and wholly a new aeon or new creation. Now, it should be conceded that theologians, with the possible exception of Rudolf Otto, have not truly succeeded in understanding a Kingdom that is simultaneously present and future, the emphasis inevitably falling upon either present or future, thereby not only distorting but losing the meaning of the Kingdom for Jesus. Crossan's distortion would appear to derive from his total emphasis upon a present Kingdom, and even if he succeeds in distancing himself from all manifest forms of realized eschatology, this is nevertheless the path of the orthodox and Catholic Church, just as, in a far more radical form, it is the way of Gnosticism, and each of these established paths is a deep threat to Crossan's goal. This is surely a fundamental reason for Crossan's deep emphasis upon the "little tradition" of an oppressed peasantry, a tradition often constituting a shadow society of structural, stylistic, and normative opposition to a ruling elite, and one apart from which Jesus' words and acts would simply be vacuous. Here, a sapiential Kingdom could only be a radical Kingdom, and if there is no wisdom tradition that actually embodies such a radicalism, it may well be just here that Jesus is and was unique.

John Dominic Crossan is a poet as well as a New Testament scholar, it has been remarked that *The Historical*

Jesus is his only book with a nonpoetic title. At the beginning of the book, when he gives us his own translation of the words of Jesus which he judges to be as close as we can get to the original language of Jesus, we encounter a language that is a universe removed from the translation of *The Five Gospels*—and we do hear a language which we can know as an enacted language. Only one primal word is rarely present in Crossan's writing: and that word is *God*. This can most dramatically be observed in the first appendix of *The Historical Jesus* where Crossan gives us his own arrangement of the Jesus tradition into complexes, and each complex contains all the attested versions of a saying or theme. He present us with 522 such complexes, each given a title by Crossan, and in only one of these titles does the word *God* appear: "God and Caesar." Perhaps no biblical scholar has ever been as careful with language as Crossan is. In this book, where he all too frequently writes "Kingdom" but only infrequently "Kingdom of God," one could almost suspect a Jewish reticence to write the divine name, or even a mystical withdrawal from an exterior name. But the truth is that a consistent avoidance of theological language now dominates New Testament scholarship, and Crossan is remarkable among his peers because he dares to employ it all, and in his book on Jesus, he does employ it at perhaps its most crucial points.

So it is that Crossan interprets the saying he inventories as "Ask, Seek, Knock," and especially in its original triadic formulation, as "a serene statement of the absolute and unmediated access to God that Jesus' movement proclaims" (p. 295). This access is present only in an "unbrokered" Kingdom, and if that is a kingdom of "nobodies," it seemingly would make manifest a God who is "nobody." Crossan never says this, indeed, he says a little as possible about God, and this despite the apparent fact that Jesus continually pronounced and enacted the name of God. In the Epilogue, which finally is at least a modest theological statement, he can say that Jesus "was neither broker nor mediator but, somewhat paradoxically, the announcer that neither should exist between humanity and divinity or between humanity and itself" (p. 422). For this is the "brokerless kingdom of God" in which miracle and parable, healing and eating, force individuals into unmediated "physical and spiritual" contact with God and with one another. No doubt the few theological statements in the Epilogue are largely a promise of future work, but decisive clues appear in his previous work, and perhaps most clearly in *Finding Is the First Act.*[6] This book itself is a dialectic of finding and seeking, exalting PLAY as the value of values, while focusing upon Jesus' treasure parable in its relation to both world treasure tales and Jewish treasure stories. Crossan finds that there is no true parallel in the world treasure tradition that goes quite as far as Jesus' "Selling All," for here and here alone the finder gives up everything, and does so with joy, to obtain the treasure of the Kingdom. But now a dark shadow appears to Crossan, for if one gives up everything, then *"one must also give up this parable itself."*[7] Thus the ultimate, most paradoxical, and most difficult demand of the Kingdom is for the abandonment of abandonment itself. Then Crossan calls up Schoenberg's own libretto to his great opera, *Moses und Aaron*, where Moses has the last word in speaking of the inconceivable and inexpressible God. This induces Crossan to return to the Exodus story of Moses and the burning bush, when God first reveals His name as "I am who I am" (Exodus 3:14). But Crossan judges this response not as an answer to Moses' request for the name of God, but rather as a refusal to answer, a declaration of unanswerability.

For Crossan this unanswerability is renewed in Jesus' parables. A biblical "aniconic" vision of God now moves from the *visually aniconic* to the *verbally aniconic,* from visual to verbal semiosis, from plastic to parabolic image. Accordingly, abandonment in the treasure parable is a paradoxical metaphor for the abandonment of parable itself. Hence Jesus' treasure parable is a "metaparable," a parable that succeeds precisely to the extent that it fails. This resolution is carried forward in Crossan's next book, *Cliffs of Fall,*[8] which is largely devoted to the parable of the sower, which it interprets as a parable about the process of parabling. Yet this parabling calls forth an eschatological but antiapocalyptic Kingdom, a Kingdom that is a permanent possibility and not an imminent certainty, for Jesus' Kingdom "derives from a radically non-apocalyptic imagination" (p. 49). And the parable of the sower is not just a parable of the Kingdom, but rather a metaparable, a parable about parables of the Kingdom. Thereby it tells us about the parabler himself. Just as the sower immediately disappears in the parable, the enactment of this parable is a deliberate self-negation of Jesus. Thus, "Jesus' text negates the sower to concentrate on the seed and thus the text and its metaphoric and polyvalent destiny take precedence over the author and will hold that primacy whether it is communicated orally or scribally" (p. 58). This is as close as Crossan ever comes to speaking positively of the crucifixion, and even if this discourse is all too indirect and elusive, it does concentrate upon the immediate disappearance of the sower, and does so once again in the context of the gift of Israel's *aniconic* monotheism.

The passion story is taken up in *The Historical Jesus* only to be historically deconstructed as prophecy become history. All too significantly it is only here that Crossan discusses either the prophetic books of the Bible or the

Dead Sea Scrolls, and examines them only to show the role they played in Mark's creation of the fictional narrative of the passion. He does concede that Jesus was crucified, and may even have foreseen his own death, but he portrays that death as having no effect whatsoever on the Kingdom Jesus embodied, which is already fully present wholly apart from the crucifixion. This, too, might well be a fundamental point at which Crossan is deeply Catholic. Just as Luther assaulted not only the Catholic Church but the Christian tradition as reversals of the Christ of Passion into the Christ of Glory, the Catholic Church deeply and dogmatically affirms that Christ's Passion did not concern or affect His Godhead (*Summa Theologica* III, 46). Crossan knows Godhead as Kingdom, and just as the Catholic Church celebrates a Godhead that is physically and spiritually present in the Eucharist, so likewise, Crossan celebrates and gives witness to Jesus' Kingdom, a Kingdom that is totally present, and totally present as a spiritual and physical presence. Not only is such a presence not a consequence of the crucifixion, it has nothing whatsoever to do with crucifixion, for even if Emmaus never happened, "Emmaus" always happens.

Nonetheless, the fact remains that in this very substantial book on the historical Jesus, Jesus is effectively bracketed from the Hebrew Bible itself, and also bracketed from the deeply apocalyptic Judaism inscribed in the Dead Sea Scrolls—which a very large number of New Testament scholars understand as the deepest historical ground both of primitive Christianity and of Jesus himself. Crossan's only manifest interest in the Old Testament is in what he regards as the northern Israelitic prophetic tradition, an ancient magical prophecy as present in Elijah and Elisha, and one which was certainly wholly transcended by the canonical prophets. Crossan has no real interest in the canonical prophets or in the prophetic revolution itself. Here he is fully united with the Jesus Seminar. How can this be possible in a genuinely historical investigation? Crossan could have learned from Max Weber himself that the reform or canonical prophets enacted an "anticultural" attack upon the whole cultural world of the ancient Near East, for civilization itself was the object of their attack.[9] Weber sees the prophetic experience as entailing no metaphysical gnosis or "interpretation of the world." All the energy of the prophet is directed to a demand for action rather than for a mystical experience or intellectual understanding, and this because of what Weber termed the "psychic economy" of the prophets, which channels all the prophets' energy into a total obedience to Yahweh (pp. 313–14). That obedience is occasioned by the imminence of a final judgment, which would destroy imperial and monarchic Israel, and historical Israel as well.

So while Crossan takes with deep seriousness the anticultural horizon of a peasant "little tradition," he has no interest in the far deeper prophetic revolution, nor any interest in recent scholarly attempts to understand the origin of Israel itself as the origin of historical revolution. Of course, this may be due in large measure to scholarly specialization, and Crossan has remarked that he has been so immersed in New Testament scholarship that he has read no systematic theology whatsoever.[10] But how could he so ignore liberation theology, and above all ignore the enormously important work of Norman K. Gottwald? Gottwald's *The Tribes of Yahweh*[11] is a comprehensive historical and sociological work that is even more substantial than *The Historical Jesus,* and it has had a comparable, if not a greater, effect, as it unveils the truly historical exodus of Israel as an exodus from an oppressive feudalistic world and the first historical occurrence of political, social, and economic revolution. Even such a mainstream scholarly work as *The Harper Atlas of the Bible* favors Gottwald's understanding of Israel's heroic age.[12] This age was launched by the first truly successful peasant uprising, one reversing an established social hierarchy even if this reversal was itself reversed by the advent of monarchic Israel. Toward the end of this stunning volume, Gottwald even offers a demythologization of Israelite Yahwism:

> "Yahweh" is the historically concretized, primordial power to establish and sustain social equality in the face of counter-oppression from without and against provincial and nonegalitarian tendencies from within the society. "The Chosen People" is the distinctive self-consciousness of a society of equals created in the intertribal order and demarcated from a primarily centralized and stratified surrounding world. "Covenant" is the bonding of decentralized social groups in a larger society of equals committed to cooperation without authoritarian leadership and a way of symbolizing the locus of sovereignty in such a society of equals. "Eschatology," or hope for the future, is sustained commitment of fellow tribesmen to a society of equals with the confidence and determination that this way of life can prevail against great environmental odds. (p. 692)

Even if this portrait is deeply idealized, it is hardly more so than Crossan's portrait of the Jesus community, and, like Crossan's portrait, it is grounded in a deep and comprehensive sociological, historical, and textual analysis.

Can Crossan ignore such a portrait because he is persuaded that Jesus' Kingdom is totally new? And is it totally new by being primordially new? Both Gottwald and Crossan are deeply opposed to utopian vision, each is interested only in a kingdom that happens here and now, and each insists upon the deep biblical ground of such a commitment. At this point, too, Crossan is a radical Catholic thinker, even as Gottwald is a radical Calvinist thinker. So, too, Crossan can find a sexual ground in primitive Christian ritual; he finds this in Secret Mark, even believing that Secret Mark is earlier than Canonical Mark, whereas the Calvinistic Gottwald sees the celebration of sex as a ruling-class luxury that is restored to its empirical ground by the revolutionary tribes of Yahweh (p. 695). Now even if both Gottwald and Crossan reveal themselves in their historical and philological quests, such self-revelation is inevitable in deep and genuine work, work which would simply be impossible apart from voyages of introspection.

No doubt this gives pause to lesser scholars, and to lesser thinkers as well, but great scholarship is inevitably radical, if only because it must sweep away so much that already has been established. We must attend to what is deeply new in the work of such scholars. Nothing is newer in *The Historical Jesus* than its full correlation, if not identification, of a sapiential and an apocalyptic Kingdom. This may very well be not only an authentic recovery of Jesus' Kingdom, but also and even precisely thereby a realization of a truly new identity of God. Yet such an identity would simultaneously be a primordial identity of God, one which has never been realized by Western theological thinking because that thinking, at least in its manifest theological forms, has never been able to escape a transcendent identity of God, a transcendence of God precluding the very possibility of primordial Godhead. Yes, Meister Eckhart did think through such a transcendence, and did call forth primordial Godhead. But Eckhart's thinking has never truly entered theological thinking, unless it did so in Hegel, Schelling, and Nietzsche.

But these are Protestant forms of theological thinking, and just as Eckhart has had little impact in the Catholic world, the Catholic world is deeply closed to that pure subject that is a primary ground of Protestant thinking, and closed if only because it is so open to the cosmos itself. There is only one truly silly remark in *The Historical Jesus*, and that is when Crossan says that the serenity communicated by Jesus derives not from knowing hidden mysteries but from watching nature's rhythms of the here and now (p. 295). Nevertheless, such an unguarded moment once again reveals a Catholic sensibility, a sensibility knowing a full union between nature and grace, and hence a genuine coinherence of the "natural" and the "supernatural." Accordingly, the Catholic can know a Creator whom the Protestant can never know, a Creator who is not only absolutely transcendent but absolutely immanent as well, and whose transcendence is inseparable from His immanence. Here, too, Crossan is deeply Augustinian, as the Protestant Augustinian cannot be, for this is a sensibility knowing a full correlation and even union between subject and Subject, or between "I" and I AM. Only on the basis of this union is there here even a possibility of the incarnation of the Body of Christ.

In this perspective, one can see even another ground for Crossan's reluctance to speak about God. For an "aniconic" monotheism could be a monotheism so deeply or primordially knowing God that it precludes the possibility of "naming" God, unless primordial naming is unnaming, or the metaparable is the dissolution of parable itself. In a deep sense, Crossan's Jesus says nothing about God, or nothing that we can hear as "God" and not even hear when the Kingdom is embodied in our very midst. Perhaps that is precisely the point at which "God" cannot be heard, and only that absence makes possible the "physical" presence of the Kingdom, a presence reversing but nevertheless thereby embodying a "spiritual" presence. Yet such a primordial presence is also and even thereby an apocalyptic presence, a presence which is truly an "ending," and an apocalyptic ending of the reversal of God that is inevitably present in the "City of Man," a City that is Antichrist itself, and that is invariably present in all hierarchy and stratification. Above all, Crossan will not dissociate the historical Jesus from a "social revolution," a revolution that is far more revolutionary than we, or even Crossan can imagine. *Commensality* is surely a weak word to use for such a revolution. So is *egalitarian commensality*, even if that is the strongest language available to us to speak of a "brokerless" Kingdom.

Is it simply impossible to say anything at all about God at this point? To speak of an unmediated access to God perhaps says something, but not if the word *God* is here unspeakable, and unspeakable if only because Crossan is clearly not speaking of anything our theologies have known as God. God is the deepest of all mysteries, our orthodox theologies continually maintain. But so long as God is simply and only a mystery, there can be no genuine and ultimate meal, and no miracle that could be a "natural" as well as a "supernatural" miracle, because it could never happen in anything that is as real to us as world. But if Jesus' Kingdom truly is a "brokerless" Kingdom, could it be the Kingdom of that God who is "Nobody," that God who is primordial Godhead, and whose total presence is precisely thereby an apocalyptic ending? Wisdom traditions the world over have known a primordial sacrality, but one that precludes any kind of historical rebellion, as most fully manifest in Gnosticism itself. This is why Crossan is even more distant from a genuine wisdom tradition than from a genuine apocalyptic tradition. If Jesus alone made those traditions one, then only here can historical revolution and primordial enlightenment go hand in hand.

CHAPTER FOUR

The Gnostic Jesus

It must always be remembered that it is not until the fourth century of the Christian era that an "orthodox" Christianity was fully established and real, not until then that there truly appears an orthodox Christ and an orthodox Christology. And this occurred only by way of the imperial power of Constantine and his court, who employed the Catholic Church as a fundamental ground of imperial order and authority. Moreover, there is no real distinction between "orthodoxy" and "heresy" in the New Testament itself. It was only in the course of the conflict with Gnosticism in the second century that Christian orthodoxy was truly born, and that birth was not actually consummated until the Constantinian era. Nothing more profoundly shaped the Catholic Church than did its ultimate struggle with Gnosticism. But now we know that this was an internal conflict within Christianity itself, perhaps the greatest civil war that has ever occurred in Christianity, and one that has been reborn once again in our own time. Certainly the discovery of the Nag Hammadi library has given us a whole new understanding of Gnosticism, and while the initial investigations of these Gnostic scriptures tended to perpetuate the ancient orthodox judgment that Gnosticism is wholly an alien heresy, more recent studies are reversing this judgment by unveiling the deep Christian ground of Gnosticism.

The most important international scholarly congress on Gnosticism occurred in the Messina Colloquium on "The Origin of Gnosticism" in 1966, which set up a committee composed of Geo Widengren, Hans Jonas, Jean Danielou, Carsten Colpe, and Ugo Bianchi, to draft a proposal for a terminological and conceptual agreement with regard to the theme of the colloquim. Although it confines itself to the Gnosticism of the second century, this proposal nevertheless declares:

> This *gnosis* of Gnosticism involves the divine identity of the *knower* (the Gnostic), the *known* (the divine substance of one's transcendent self), and the *means by which one knows* (*gnosis* as an implicit divine faculty is to be awakened and actualized). This *gnosis* is a revelation-tradition of a different type from the Biblical and Islamic revelation-tradition.[1]

There were certainly scholars, even at that colloquium, who thought otherwise, as recorded by one of its major participants, James M. Robinson.[2] One of its published papers declares, "It is probable that what eventually became the 'orthodox' and the 'heretical' traditions continued for some time side by side, mutually influencing one another, before the lines of division became distinct."[3] Yet to judge by the published papers and discussion, Hans Jonas was the most powerful figure at this colloquium, and it is Jonas who has given us the fullest philosophical and historical understanding of Gnosticism.

Perhaps Jonas's most important thesis is that Gnosticism is the most radical or revolutionary movement in the ancient world, one that not only reversed classical culture but "shattered the panlogistical or pantheistic illusion of the ancient world."[4] For Jonas, the Gnostics were the first speculative theologians in the "new age" of religion superseding classical antiquity, and they created the ideas of an antidivine universe, of humanity's alienness within it, and of the acosmic nature of the Godhead. Thereby they also created the first mythical-speculative history of descending emanations from the primordial Godhead. Jonas thinks that there are two systems of Gnosticism, Iranian and Syrian—the one a pure dualism of two opposed principles, and the other deriving dualism itself from the one and undifferentiated source of all—both revolving about an inner divine "devolution," and both embodying an ultimate tragedy within Godhead itself:

> Both dramas start with a disturbance in the heights; in both, the existence of the world marks a discomfiture of the divine and a necessary, in itself undesirable, means of an eventual restoration; in both, the salvation of man is that of the deity itself. The difference lies in whether the tragedy of the deity is forced upon it from outside, with Darkness having the first initiative, or is motivated from within itself, with Darkness the product of its passion, not its cause. To divine defeat and sacrifice in the one case, corresponds divine guilt and error in the other; to compassion for the victimized Light— spiritual contempt of demiurgical blindness; to eventual divine liberation—reformation through enlightenment.[5]

This motif is carried forward in Jonas's Messina paper, but now it is deepened in terms of the time axis of the Gnostic world, a progressive and dynamic movement of time, embodying a total evolution: "It is a metaphyics of

pure movement and event, the most determinedly 'historical' conception of universal being prior to Hegel (with whom
it also shares the axiom—implicit in the ontological status
of knowledge—that 'substance is subject')."[6] Nevertheless,
the metaphysics of Gnosticism is a mythical metaphysics—that is essential to its nature. Here the transcendence
of the supreme deity is stressed to the utmost degree, and
yet the Absolute is not alone, but is surrounded by an aura
of eternal and hierarchical expressions of its infinitude,
and it is from these that the downward movement breach-
ing the self-containment of the divine realm occurs. This
is that cosmic process of the "devolution" of deity that a
uniquely Gnostic redemption reverses. That redemption is
not only the salvation of the elect, but also the instrument
for the reintegration of the impaired Godhead itself, or
"the selfsaving of God."[7] Jonas finds this Gnostic theme to
be truly original historically, and while he is disturbed by
the unmistakably "secondhand" and artificial means of its
mythical expressions, there can be no doubt of its deep
and profound power in its own world. Nothing is more
primal here than the fall of deity or Godhead itself, and
Jonas believes that even Plotinus succumbed to Gnosticism at this point, being impelled by his own thinking to
accept a fall of the universal Soul through cosmogonic
agency, whereas Plato knew only the Orphic myth of the
fall of individual souls into bodies.[8]

The most significant development in Gnostic scholarship since the Messina colloquium has been a truly new
understanding of primitive Christian Gnosticism. This has
been largely inspired not only by the Gospel of Thomas
and the Thomas tradition itself, but also by a new understanding of a very early "wisdom" or Sophia Christianity,
which Crossan and others understand as having been initiated by Jesus himself. Significantly, James M. Robinson

was Permanent Secretary of the International Committee for the Nag Hammadi Codices, the group that published *The Facsimile Edition of the Nag Hammadi Codicies*. For more than forty years Robinson has been deeply involved with the International Q Project, thereby engaged in bridging if not dissolving the gulf between early Q and the Gospel of Thomas. Robinson's essay "LOGOI SOPHON" initiated the scholarly correlation of Thomas and Q. Yet it is Helmut Koester's *Ancient Christian Gospels*[9] which has given a virtually canonical status to this new perspective, and in its Preface Koester states that the epithets "heretical" and "orthodox" are meaningless for the description of the history and development of gospel literature in the earliest period of Christianity (p. xxx). Koester affirms that there are full parallels between many of the sayings in early Q and in the Gospel of Thomas, showing that Thomas had full access to the traditions that formed the basis of Q's composition. Koester also argues that Thomas preserved forms of the sayings and parables of Jesus that are more original than the forms that are extant in the common sayings source of Matthew and Luke (p. 97).

Koester also believes that the Gospel of Thomas and the Gospel of John employ the same traditions, but he thinks that the Johannine "I am" sayings were created by the author of the Fourth Gospel as an anti-Gnostic device, which was fundamental to the Gospel of John's assault upon an early Christian "Gnosticizing" of salvation (p. 263). There are only two "I am" sayings in Thomas, but one is deeply and purely Gostic, which Koester translates as "It is I who am the all" (77a). This saying parallels a number of wisdom sayings in Thomas that speak of a divine Wisdom who invites human beings to follow her in order to find true life, such as: "Come unto me, for my yoke is easy and my lordship is mild, and you will find repose for yourselves" (Koester's translation of Gos. Thom. 90). Moreover, Koester is also persuaded that Paul's assault upon his opponents in I Corinthians 1–4 is not only an opposition to early Christian Gnosticism, but a violent response to a "Wisdom" salvation tradition, for "Wisdom" sayings of Jesus must have been the vehicle on the basis of which the Corinthians claimed to have received this salvation" (p. 60). Accordingly, within a generation after the death of Jesus, a genuine Christian Gnosticism had been born, one employing a radical myth of Wisdom. Koester assures us that the myth of Wisdom is always docetic, because she is never really human and her followers' ultimate identity is not human but divine (p. 271). Certainly the Gnostic Jesus is a docetic Jesus throughout the history of Gnosticism. If that divine Wisdom is as early as any Jesus in the recorded Christian tradition, then there must have been a very early and revolutionary Christian response to the crucifixion.

While once it was thought that there is an overwhelming gulf between early Christianity and the mature Gnosticism of the second century, now it is commonly thought that there are deep links between the Thomas tradition and Valentinian Gnosticism, and it is the school of Valentinus which apparently was the most powerful Gnosticism of the second and third centuries. Indeed, even Sethian Gnosticism can know Jesus as the incarnation of a preexistent Seth or Christ. The truth is, there are no Gnostic texts known to us that can be wholly dissociated from Christianity, so that to speak of an actual historical Gnosticism is to speak of a deep expression of Christianity itself. Of course, Valentinus and Marcion were contemporaries, and each had a profound affect upon the Catholic Church, and so much so that the Catholic Church and Christian orthodoxy are inconceivable apart from them.

Here it is that the biblical God is most deeply known as the alien God, alien above all insofar as the biblical God is the Creator, but likewise alien insofar as the biblical God is the source of Torah or Law, a Law that has enslaved humanity even as the creation has imprisoned our eternal souls. Jonas consistently opposed a Jewish origin of Gnosticism, and there are few scholars who adhere to that thesis today. So now that there appears to be no alternative to a Christian origin of Gnosticism, that origin demands a genuine theological investigation.

The Gospel of Truth, a title given it by modern scholars, was very probably written by Valentinus himself. It opens with the proclamation of the truth for those who have received grace from the "Father of truth," that they might learn to know Him through the power of the Logos that emanated from the spiritual universe that is in the Father's thought and intellect. The Logos is the Savior, a Savior who is necessary inasmuch as the totality of spiritual reality, a totality that had emanated from the Father (16:4), had searched in vain for its origin but its search was wholly blocked by the material universe, which is itself a consequence of "error." Forgetfulness for the origin arose because the Father was unknown. But now the "perfect" can know their origin:

> It is to the perfect that this, the proclamation of the one they search for, has made itself known, through the mercies of the father. By this the hidden mystery Jesus Christ shed light upon those who were, because of forgetfulness, in darkness. He enlightened them and gave them a way, and the way is the truth, about which he instructed them. For this reason error became angry at him and persecuted him. She was constrained by him, and became

inactive. He was nailed to a tree and became fruit
of the father's acquaintance. (18:11-26)[10]

The Savior is the fruit of the Father's *gnosis*. Whoever eats
that fruit knows the Father, thereby forgetfulness is wholly
dissolved, and a spiritual totality can return to its origin.

The Gospel of Truth is at some distance from Jonas's
schema, and perhaps most so in so centering upon Jesus,
and not only upon Jesus but even upon the crucifixion:

> Since the father of the entirety is invisible—and the
> entity derives from him, from whom every way
> emanated—Jesus appeared, wrapped himself in that
> document, was nailed to a piece of wood, and pub-
> lished the father's edict upon the cross. O, such a
> great lesson! Drawing himself down into death,
> clothed in eternal life, having put off the corrupt
> rags, he put on incorruptibility, a thing that no one
> can take from him. (20:19-34)[11]

For the Father's secret is His Son, and the name of the
Father is the Son (38:6), that Son by whom alone the Father can be known, a knowledge that is an absolute return
from forgetfulness to that Father who is all in all.

In *The Gospel of Truth* the fall is quite simply forgetfulness, a cosmic forgetfulness that is the very creation of the
world, and the material universe passes into nothingness
when the Father is truly known. So it is that even if Jesus
is crucified, he thereby put on incorruptibility, thereby
destroying the darkness of forgetfulness. Here, and quite
commonly in Valentinianism, the crucifixion is docetic,
an illusory appearance, or, as *The Gospel According to
Philip* declares:

> Those who say that the lord first died and then
> arose are mistaken, for he first arose and then died.
> If one does not first get resurrection, one will not
> die. As god lives! that person would. (56:15)[12]

Thus the crucifixion is resurrection, even as it is in the
Fourth Gospel. But unlike the Fourth Gospel, the Gnostic
Jesus is wholly docetic, and in no sense whatsoever a genuine human being. Nevertheless, the name of the Father is
the Son, a consistent motif in Valentinianism, a name
which finally brings an end to the cosmic universe. According to St. Clement, this is something concrete that
Valentinus said about Jesus:

> He was continent, enduring all things. Jesus digested
> divinity; he ate and drank in a special way, without
> excreting his solids. He had such a great capacity for
> continence that the nourishment within him was
> not corrupted, for he did not experience corruption.[13]

Perhaps that is as concrete an image of the docetic Jesus as
is possible, but the fact remains that the Valentinians could
know a crucified Jesus who is a docetic Jesus, and could
even make that Jesus the center of their proclamation.

But is this so far from the Gospel of Thomas? In the
Thomas tradition, Jesus is known only through "Thomas,"
the twin of Jesus, and in *The Book of Thomas*, Thomas is
explicitly called Jesus' "brother" and "double" (138:7f.,
138:19f.). All too naturally, such a double can know and
proclaim only a purely heavenly Jesus, and so heavenly
that this Jesus is never associated with passion and death.
Is it possible that the Thomas tradition becomes even more
deeply Christian in Valentinian Gnosticism? Certainly a

cosmic redemption is real in Valentinianism but is apparently absent in the Thomas tradition, and if this parallels an early Christian apocalypticism, it does so most clearly in knowing the end of the world. Ptolemy was one of Valentinus's first and most brilliant students, and according to Irenaeus this is how he could describe Wisdom's passionate search:

> The lord came to his passion "at the last times" of the world—they say—so as to manifest the passion that occurred with the last day of the aeons, and so that the end of the affairs of the aeons might be reflected in his end.[14]

Here, crucifixion is not only resurrection, but apocalypse as well, an apocalypse that is not only the end of the world, but the end of every spirit that has not fully and wholly returned to its primordial union with the Father. While this is surely deification, it is not unlike that deification which became so powerful in ancient Eastern Christianity, and that has been renewed again and again in the deepest expressions of Christian mysticism.

Such deification is finally inseparable from an apprehension of the Creator as the alien God. Although this motif is muted in *The Gospel of Truth*, this proclamation may well be the earliest surviving sermon of Christian mysticism, as Bentley Layton believes,[15] a sermon wherein every word is directed to the realization of an ultimate goal. Certainly that goal entails the dissolution of the Creator, a Creator who would inevitably disappear with the passage of the material universe into nothingness, and the deepest symbol of that passage is the cross. That is why the Son is the name of the Father. The perfect can know that name only as deification, even as the predestination of the perfect is finally realized in deification. Virtually all scholars are agreed that the goal of Gnosticism is deification, but in the more elaborate Gnostic myths this goal is initially manifest through an epiphany of the Creator as Satan. The dominant Gnostic name of Satan is Ialdabaoth, the first and chief ruler of the visible universe. In the *Apocryphon of John*, Ialdabaoth declares: "It is I who am god, and no other god exists apart from me" (11:21).[16] Clearly this is a parody of the God of Exodus, but a parody intending to call forth the biblical God as Satan, and nothing is a deeper barrier to deification than the biblical God. Thus the Creator is not only the alien God but the enemy God, an enemy whose name is Ialdabaoth or Satan, just as deification is inseparable from the annihilation of the world.

So, too, Jesus' body could not possibly be a physical body, just as Jesus' crucifixion could not possibly be a physical death, for death is not possible for pure spirit, and is at bottom an illusion that the perfect are called upon to forget. Yet something very like this was apparently believed by Paul's Corinthian opponents, who claimed to live only in the Christ of glory, and who could repudiate the crucifixion. So likewise the Johannine adversaries of the second epistle of John, whom the Presbyter can speak of as Antichrists, refuse to confess "Jesus Christ coming in the flesh."[17] Valentinian Gnostics could accept the flesh and blood of Jesus only insofar as "flesh" means the Word, and "blood" means the holy spirit (*The Gospel According to Philip* 57:6). Certainly this is a purely spiritual Christianity, but one which is in some genuine continuity with very early expressions of Christianity, so that it is now possible to apprehend a historical trajectory of Christian Gnosticism from the first century to the second century and beyond. Even though Christian orthodoxy could know

Gnosticism as an alien heresy, that orthodoxy only came into existence by way of a deep conflict with Christian Gnosticism, and it inevitably bears the imprints of that conflict.

A decisive clue as to both the genesis and the deep ground of Christian orthodoxy lies in its understanding of redemption. In fourth-century orthodoxy, redemption was in some sense deification, a deification that is possible only by way of union with the full deity of Christ. Already in the Second Epistle of Peter, which was probably sent from the church of Rome about 80–90 C.E., we find this claim for "Jesus our Lord":

> His divine power has given us everything needed for life and godliness, through the knowledge of him who called us by his own glory and goodness. Thus he has given us, through these things, his precious and very great promises, so that through them you may escape from the corruption that is in the world because of lust, and may become participants of the divine nature. (2 Peter 1:3f., NRSV)

All too significantly, this epistle was written in response to doubts about the Lord's coming. Scoffers scorn that coming because everything continues as it has since the beginning of creation, leading the author of this early encyclical to insist that with the Lord one day is like a thousand years: "But the day of the Lord will come like a thief, and then the heavens will pass away with a loud noise, and the elements will be dissolved with fire, and the earth and everything that is done on it will be disclosed" (2 Peter 3:10, NRSV).

This will be the last time that Peter's apostolic authority will be employed to proclaim an apocalyptic ending, for within a generation of this encyclical an original Christian apocalyptic hope had withered away, and a nascent Catholic Church was deeply engaged in a radical process of "de-eschatologizing" the dominant expressions of the original gospel.[18] But this had already occurred at virtually the beginning of Christianity, as is most clearly manifest in the Gospel of Thomas and perhaps also in the earliest stratum of Q, and surely both in Corinthian Gnosticism and in that Gnosticism which so profoundly divided the Johannine community. Yet a radical de-eschatologizing occurred in Christian Gnosticism before it occurred in those ecclesiastical traditions that were in process of becoming the Catholic Church. We know that the latter violently reacted against the former, and that this reaction deepened in the second century, so it cannot be accidental that both Christian Gnosticism and Christian "orthodoxy" alike engaged in de-eschatologizing. No doubt this process was far deeper in Gnosticism. From its very beginning Gnosticism had only known a realized eschatology, and there are very good reasons to believe that Gnosticism itself created "realized eschatology." Moreover, a realized eschatology can most clearly appear as deification, for believers are here summoned not only to become united with a divine Wisdom, but to pass into that Wisdom itself, thereby returning to their heavenly origin. This is just the pattern which is manifest in the Gospel of Thomas, and if the Gospel of Thomas embodies the purest realized eschatology in early Christian writing, realized eschatology is here clearly inseparable from deification.

Work has only just begun upon attempting to assess the impact of Gnosticism upon a mature Christian orthodoxy, but there can be little doubt that this impact occurred, and perhaps most deeply so in orthodox Christology itself. Athanasius could insist upon the full and substantial deity of Christ because otherwise redemption would be impossible, a redemption which can even be understood as divinisation, as it was by Irenaeus himself, who was the foremost orthodox opponent of Gnosticism:

> Irenaeus formulated for posterity, in an impressive and authoritative manner, the following thesis, which was of fundamental importance for doctrine: "Thus he (through the Incarnation) mixed together and intermingled the Spirit of the Father with the creature of God, so Man might be after the image and similitude of God." The divine Logos had "by his immeasurable love freely become what we are, in order that he might make us what he is." Athanasius had spoken to a similar effect: the divine Logos himself "had become Man, so that we might become divine."[19]

Certainly the paradigmatic formula that God became man in order that man might become God is extraordinarily powerful in ancient Christian orthodoxy, and above all so after the second and third centuries, those centuries which mark the high point of Gnosticism in the ancient world. So that if it is Gnosticism which most deeply and most purely centers upon the ultimate goal of deification, at the very least there is a genuine trace of this goal in Christian orthodoxy, and that as early as the Second Epistle of Peter.

Now just as symbols of the cross are virtually absent from ancient Christian iconography, the crucifixion itself first disappears in primitive Christian Gnosticism, and then reappears in Gnosticism only as a docetic or illusory death, a death disguising the eternal and divine identity of the perfect. But we must never lose sight of Jonas's thesis that Gnosticism is the most radical movement in the ancient

world. It was surely radical in its goal of an absolute deification, a deification going far beyond the Hellenistic
mystery cults in seeking a total union with the fullness of
primordial Godhead itself. That even Plotinus could em-
brace this goal is extraordinarily significant, and if it was
the Gnostics who created a theology revolving about the
emanations of primordial Godhead, and one accepted by
Plotinus himself, then those emanations are a decisive key
to a uniquely Gnostic deification, a deification which is an
absolute return to an unfallen pleroma. Absolute return is
the deepest movement of the Gnostic way. This is the
very essence of *gnosis* itself, and it is inseparable from the
fall of the Godhead. Even if that fall is finally illusory, it
is inseparable from the deepest and purest expression of
Gnostic *praxis*, a *praxis* which is nothing less than an
absolute deification. No such deification would be possible
apart from the fall or emanation of the Godhead, and just
as Gnosticism whether implicitly or explicitly assaults or
dissolves the biblical Creator, that dissolution or assult is
inseparable from a uniquely Gnostic goal. And if we can
now be confident that Gnosticism has its origin in the
earliest expressions of Christianity, then the Gnostic goal
of absolute return cannot be dissociated from a uniquely
Christian redemption.

   Quite possibly it was Christian Gnostics who first knew
Jesus as a fully divine redeemer. Here there is a deep dividing line between Gnosticism and the synoptic, Pauline,
and Johannine traditions, traditions finally refusing a purely
docetic Jesus, thereby refusing not only a purely docetic
redeemer but also a purely docetic redemption. This is
clear above all in the primacy of the crucifixion in these
traditions, and not a "spiritual" crucifixion, but a crucifixion which is a real and actual death. Now even if that
death is finally life, a crucifixion which is resurrection, it

nevertheless is remembered and recalled as death itself, and not a docetic death but a death that occurred in the fullness of historical actuality. Nothing is further from Gnosticism than any kind of historical awareness whatsoever, an absence that is already decisive in the Gospel of Thomas, and it continues throughout the history of Gnosticism, and so much so that even a substantial Gnostic library failed to reveal any historical or even biographical data. Not only is this in striking contrast to the Dead Sea Scrolls, but also to the New Testament itself, and nothing more clearly distinguishes canonical from Gnostic scripture. But if the life of the perfect is a docetic or "spiritual" life, we should expect just such an abatement of all worldly consciousness, at least in its scriptural expressions. And once again we can see a deep Gnostic ground for an opposition to the Bible, for the Hebrew Bible is the most fully historical scripture in the world.

Yet is it possible to understand a uniquely Gnostic Godhead as "the selfsaving of God"? If so, is it possible to understand such a Godhead as the Crucified God? Many scholars have called attention to a presumed radical lifestyle of the Gnostics—a lifestyle that is fully paralleled in the earliest Christian communities, and is not simply ascetic but embraces death itself as life. Such a lifestyle was apparently absent in the Qumran community, even as it is absent from all the multiple expressions of the Biblical tradition or traditions, so at this point, too, a radical way of Wisdom was a deep historical innovation. But if that innovation occurs immediately after the crucifixion, and is even a response to Jesus himself, then that divine tragedy of which Jonas speaks cannot be dissociated from the Jesus who is known in faith, and above all known as having been crucified under Pontius Pilate. Certainly Gnosticism knows a fully divine redeemer, and does so in its earliest expressions, and if those expressions occurred so soon after the crucifixion, it is difficult to imagine that they were not deep responses to the crucifixion itself. And therefore responses to the Crucified God? Does the crucifixion initiate an absolute return to the Godhead, a return made possible only by the death of the divine Redeemer, a death first truly reversing the fall of the Godhead and yet occurring in Godhead itself? Of course, for Gnosticism that death is eternal life. But only now is that life enacted or revealed, and enacted in a Jesus who is not only the divine Wisdom but the fullness of deity itself.

Certainly at this crucial point a primitive or original Gnosticism is at an immense distance from the whole horizon of the Hebrew Bible, and likewise distant from all known forms of Jewish apocalypticism. Even if Galilee was very much under the influence of Hellenistic culture, there is no evidence whatsoever for a pre-Christian radical mysticism in the Hellenistic world. Gnosticism truly is a revolutionary mysticism, and it is manifestly a Christian revolution, occurring almost immediately in Christian history. But just as much later expressions of radical Christian mysticism, such as those which occurred in Meister Eckhart and in William Blake, are most radical in their visions of God, a God who finally dissolves or is self-annihilated as "God," so, too, Gnosticism was most radical in its visions of the Godhead. Gnosticism's Godhead not only is all in all, but it can be manifest as such only when it is wholly realized within, so that to know that Godhead is to be Godhead itself. That is the very essence of a uniquely Gnostic *gnosis*. True, such a *gnosis* existed long before this in India, but there is no evidence for its prior existence in the Mediterranean world, and if Gnosticism is a revolutionary transformation of the biblical tradition, that is a revolution which first occurs among followers of Jesus.

Yet there is no image whatsoever of a "selfsaving" God in India or the Orient, no vision or tradition of a deity or a primordial totality that enacts or realizes a redemption of itself, just as there are no visions there of an original "fall," or certainly not in the uniquely Gnostic and Christian sense of fall. In mature Gnosticism, the fall is the fall of a primordial pleroma or totality. Even if it is finally an illusory fall, it is inseparable from the Gnostic way of absolute return and a uniquely Gnostic deification. Gnostics know that deification as being embodied, even uniquely embodied, in Jesus, a Jesus who is the Savior only insofar as Jesus is fully divine, and that divinity itself is the very embodiment of the pleroma. Can the Gnostic Jesus be understood as the "selfsaving God"? As that God, and that unique God, that enacts a redemption of itself, a redemption that is finally the redemption of the pleroma? Could this be an ultimate response to the crucifixion itself, a crucifixion which is the passion and death of the divine Redeemer, but which issues in the resurrection of all? Did the earliest Christian Gnostics refuse the crucifixion because they could know crucifixion only as resurrection itself, a resurrection finally ending the world as world? And is a purely docetic Jesus a Jesus who is the fruit of that victory, that redemption of the pleroma which is possible only by way of the redemption of Godhead itself?

In this perspective, one could see orthodox Christianity as a deeply muted or transformed Gnosticism, one wholly repudiating even the possibility of the redemption of the Godhead, and knowing a redemption that is wholly independent of the world as world, thus sanctioning a creation that is independent of redemption, and a Christ who is simultaneously the fullness of the Godhead and the fullness of a wholly creaturely humanity. Then only humanity is redeemed; the redemption has no effect whatsoever upon God as God, who is and only is an absolutely immutable and ineffable God. Thereby the passion and death of God is only the suffering and death of the humanity of Christ, for while the Son of God underwent a real death, Christ died as man and not as God. This ancient Christian orthodoxy is reborn in Thomas Aquinas in a fully systematic form, and Aquinas can know the Incarnation as not affecting the absolute immutability of God in any way, although it does effect the "deification" of the elect:

> As Damascene says, the Divine Nature is said to be incarnate because it is united to flesh personally, and not that it is changed into flesh. So likewise the flesh is said to be deified, as he also says, not by change, but by union with the Word, its natural properties still remaining, and hence it may be considered as deified, inasmuch as it becomes the flesh of the Word of God, but not that it becomes God. (*Summa Theologica* III, 2, 1).[20]

Flesh is a technical term here for the whole man, a humanity that is redeemed or deified through union with Christ, and union with the passion of Christ. That passion does not affect Christ's divine or higher powers, or even his "higher reason," but only the lower or temporal powers of the incarnate Christ (III, 46, 7).[21]

Thus Christian orthodoxy knows a Redeemer who suffers and dies only in his humanity or human nature. The divine nature of Christ is wholly unaffected by his death, and redemption can be the redemption only of a fallen humanity. Redemption occurs through the body of Christ, an incarnate body, composed of inferior elements: "Therefore the body of Christ was not a heavenly but a carnal and earthly body" (III, 5, 2).[22] Accordingly, an orthodox anti-docetism can know the crucifixion not as the death of God, but only as the death of Christ's carnal body, and although that death does effect redemption, it has no effect whatsoever upon God as God. Certainly this is a deeply anti-Gnostic orthodoxy, and perhaps most deeply anti-Gnostic in so fully affirming that redemption can in no way whatsoever affect God himself, a God who is absolutely immutable and impassive, absolutely unaffected by the suffering and death of Christ. Thereby Christ is wholly divided in his human and divine natures, and while Christ is God made man, and even "God truly humanized" (III, 2, 6),[23] the union of the divine and human natures is a union occurring only in the "person" or the individual substance of the incarnate Christ, and not one which is truly present in His passion and death. Here, a Gnostic Christ of glory is wholly negated, thus preserving the individual Jesus, but only at the cost of dissolving redemption as an act of God, or even as an act in which God as God is present and real.

While Christian orthodoxy can be apprehended as a reversal of Gnosticism, it is a reversal made possible by Gnosticism itself, and above all made possible by the totality of a uniquely Gnostic redemption. Christianity may well be the most revolutionary movement in history, but it is first a revolution within Christianity itself. If Christianity is revolutionary in its vision and understanding of God, that could only be by way of an apprehension of the totality of God, a totality first known by Gnosticism. As opposed to Oriental vision, this is a dynamic and even forward moving totality. This occurs through the emanations of the Godhead, these emanations are consummated in what the Christian knows as incarnation, crucifixion, and resurrection, a resurrection that is a total resurrection, and therefore a resurrection affecting Godhead itself. It is just by refusing this uniquely Gnostic resurrection that Christian orthodoxy realized itself. But only thereby could Christian orthodoxy know the absolutely immutable and ineffable God, a God who is absolute impassivity, and thereby and only thereby the absolutely transcendent God. That is a transcendence that Gnosticism not only opposed, but absolutely assaulted in its visions of the Creator as Satan. The very majesty and absolutely sovereign power of the Creator are the deepest barriers to Gnostic redemption, a uniquely Gnostic redemption which is not only deification, but even an absolute deification, a deification embodying Godhead itself. If the reversal of that deification is the realization of Christian orthodoxy, that is a realization impossible apart from Gnostic deification, and impossible apart from the Gnostic Jesus, a Jesus who is the totality of Godhead itself, but a totality that presents itself as being a redemptive totality in the Gnostic Jesus.

CHAPTER FIVE

The Pauline Jesus

There is only one individual in the world of early Christianity whom we can know as an individual, and that is Paul, the first writer in antiquity to record his own uniquely individual "I" or self-consciousness, and the first theologian in Christianity, if not the first truly individual theologian in the world. No figure in the ancient world is more controversial than Paul, a Paul who could not only engage in a violent struggle with the apostolic leaders of the Jewish Christian Church, but who could apparently subordinate the early Jesus traditions themselves to his own absolute and apostolic authority and who could even confess: "Therefore, to keep me from being too elated, a thorn was given me in the flesh, a messenger of Satan to torment me" (2 Corinthians 12:7 NRSV). Paul was deeply controversial not only in his own world, but also in those Christian centuries which succeeded him, and perhaps most so in the second century C.E., when Gnostic and Catholic theologians alike claimed Pauline authority, and when Pauline exegesis was torn asunder by these polar forces. James M. Robinson has identified a gradual bifurcation in the earliest Pauline tradition, and one impelling a dichotomous historical trajectory, "with one stream moving via Ephesians to I Peter, Luke-Acts, the Pastorals, and on to orthodoxy, the other via Colossians to Valentinus, Basilides, Marcion, and on to heresy."[1] But this radical trajectory parallels an equally radical trajectory from an "unworldly" apocalyptic Christianity to a relatively "worldly" Christian establishment, and Robinson confesses that a new understanding of the historical trajectories of early Christianity evolved out of a categorical crisis in New Testament scholarship itself.

Paul's relation to the Jesus traditions he inherited has long been problematic, as has been his crucial distinction between the Jesus "according to the Spirit" and the Jesus "according to the flesh." Bultmann is representative of the dominant scholarly judgment that after his conversion Paul made no effort to contact Jesus' disciples or the Jerusalem Church to be instructed about Jesus, and his letters barely show traces of the influence of Palestinian traditions concerning Jesus, for all that is important to him in the story of Jesus is that he was born a Jew and lived under the Law and had then been crucified. He quotes "Words of the Lord" only rarely, and then only so as to regulate church life. Even when Paul refers to Christ as an example, he is thinking not of the historical but of the preexistent Jesus (Philippians 2:5ff.; 2 Corinthians 8:9; Romans 15:3).[2] Yet Bultmann also believes that the Kingdom of God, which was fundamental in the eschatological proclamation and the teaching of Jesus, has lost its dominant role in Paul. Here we encounter a deep polarization in twentieth-century New Testament scholarship, one revolving about a division between an apocalyptic interpretation, as inspired by Schweitzer, and a demythologizing and "existential" interpretation, as inspired by Bultmann. Of course, Bultmann follows Schweitzer and Weiss in maintaining that the historical Jesus was an apocalyptic prophet of the Kingdom of God, but he created a radical hermeneutic in which an apocalyptic Kingdom is most deeply an existential Word, a demythologizing that he found already in the Fourth Gospel, but that is first recorded in the kerygmatic language of Paul.

Many of Bultmann's conservative critics have judged that his demythologizing is a modern renewal or rebirth of ancient Gnostic exegesis. There surely are remarkable parallels between them, and perhaps most clearly so a dichotomy between the fleshly Jesus and the spiritual Christ. This is not a dialectical dichotomy in which "flesh" and "spirit" pass into each other, but rather an ultimate and unbridgeable dichotomy. And just as Bultmann has been the most creative and influential interpreter of the New Testament in the twentieth century, much the same could be said of the Valentinian Gnostics of the second century, who had a deep effect upon the rapidly developing Catholic Church, as witness the defensive but violent assaults upon them by Irenaeus, Tertullian, and Origen. As Elaine Pagels has most clearly demonstrated in *The Gnostic Paul*,[3] the Valentinians and other Gnostics divided humanity into three predestined groups: the "hylics," who will finally altogether be destroyed; the "psychics," or lower Christians, whose final destiny is problematic; and the "pneumatics," who are already fully redeemed or resurrected. The Valentinians regarded Paul as their founding apostle, one to whom the psychic or Catholic Peter is wholly subordinated, and Paul is the apostle of an absolute freedom, which is not only a freedom from the Law of the demiurge or the Creator, but also a freedom released by the crucified and resurrected Christ. So it is that the Valentinians could understand Paul's affirmation that he has "died" to the Law in the epistle to the Galatians as a pneumatic redemption from the cosmos and its demiurgic ruler. For in crucifixion, the cosmos has been crucified to me, and "I" to the cosmos (Galatians 6:14), so that what was bodily or hylic in Paul has been consumed, what is psychic has been purified, and he now lives pneumatically, or, rather, Christ lives "in him" (p. 106).

Nothing is more elusive in Gnosticism than Sophia, a Sophia who is the Mother of us all, and whose own rebellious passion not only initiated the fall but is consummated in the crucifixion. Although Paul's letters are silent about such a Sophia, the Valentinians understand Paul's subordination of women to be a subordination of psychics, for Eve in being separated from Adam became the lower psychic element. But the creation of Eve was the creation of Sophia herself, and it is through Sophia that Christ and the elect are generated into the cosmos.[4] Even though such generation is fall, it is nevertheless reversed in crucifixion, a crucifixion which is not only a renewal of the passion of Sophia, but its full and final reversal. Now just as nothing is so primal in Paul as is the crucifixion of Christ, that crucifixion is the reversal of the cosmos itself in Valentinian exegesis, and its consummation will be the destruction of the demiurge's "kingdom of death," so that "God may be all in all" (I Corinthians 15:28).

There is a genuinely kenotic or self-emptying motif in Valentinian theology. Not only did Jesus willingly allow himself to be divided to restore the fallen elect into the unity of the primordial pleroma, but Jesus emptied himself of light and came into existence outside of the limit of the pleroma in the place of emptiness, *kenoma*:

> When he came into the cosmos, "through great humility he appeared not as an angel but as a man." According to the Interpretation of the Gnosis, the savior says: "I became very small, so that through my humility I might bring you up to my great height. . . . if you will believe in me, it is I who will bring you above by means of this form *(schema)* which you see." For he who "put on" the psychic Christ, and finally even the bodily form of Jesus ("taking on the form of a slave, coming to be in the

likeness of men"—Phil. 2:7), in order to become humanly visible.[5]

However, that kenotic incarnation is an incarnation of the pleroma.[6] If it is fulfilled in the crucifixion, a new humanity is thereby created, and a humanity which is not only a resurrected humanity, but a new humanity that is apocalypse itself.

It is truly remarkable that there are so many parallels between Christian Gnosticism and Christian apocalypticism. Both go back to the very beginnings of Christianity, so each might well be inseparable from the other, as would appear to be true in twentieth-century New Testament hermeneutics. Schweitzer's apocalyptic interpretation of Jesus and Paul has been deeply renewed during the past generation, particularly under the impact of the Dead Sea Scrolls. Most New Testament scholars understand Jesus to have arisen out of the world of Jewish apocalypticism, and many, if not most, Pauline scholars now understand Paul as being profoundly apocalyptic, thereby bridging an apparent gulf between Jesus and Paul. Schweitzer, in the Preface to his great book on Paul, *The Mysticism of Paul the Apostle*,[7] confesses that this work brings a conclusion to his earlier work on Jesus (p. viii) and if Paul's apocalyptic and mystical doctrine of redemption has not been taken up into Church dogma, that dogma effected a bifurcation between Christ and ethical *praxis* that is impossible in a Pauline dying and rising again with Christ. Now it is not insignificant that Schweitzer the disciple so deeply followed the call of Jesus, and only after many years as a medical missionary in Africa did he complete his book on Paul, and this is a book not only of a scholar but of a follower, and a follower not only of Jesus but also of Paul. That gives this book an authority found in no other study of Paul, and only here is a Pauline ethics so deeply called forth.

While Schweitzer's employment of a mystical language in interpreting Paul has offended many, he makes it all too clear that a Pauline mystical "being-in-Christ" is radically different from a "God-mysticism" or a mystical deification. Paul's is a Christ-mysticism, a real "co-experiencing" of crucifixion and resurrection, from which ethics itself directly and immediately results (p. 295). Moreover, Schweitzer carefully distinguishes a mystical "being-in-Christ" from a mystical rebirth, the latter appearing in the deutero-Pauline literature, and then coming to dominate the Johannine tradition and early Logos theology. Such rebirth is isolated from ethics, and it wholly lacks the realism of an authentically Pauline call, for that call issues from the fruits of resurrection, and is inseparable from the real and actual advent of the new aeon. New Testament interpreters who can understand apocalypse only as a future reality are clearly alienated from Paul. For Paul the crucifixion and the resurrection of Christ are the triumphant advent of the Kingdom of God, and precisely this apocalyptic ground is embodied in a new ethical life. So that an "interim ethics" that Schweitzer discovered in Jesus is now reborn, but reborn only with the ending of every real interim between now and then, for now apocalypse is far more a present than a future reality.

Schweitzer believes that for John the Baptist, for Jesus, and for primitive Christianity the whole of ethics falls under repentance, or *metanoia*. But for Paul ethics no longer is, nor can be, repentance, and cannot be for it proceeds from a mystical being-in-Christ. Here Schweitzer and Bultmann are very close, each transforming the distinction between the indicative and the imperative. But for Schweitzer this transformation is inseparable from an apoca-

lyptic ground, for the advent of apocalypse is the ending of
a world that *is* world, so that being "not as the world" in
action is the expression of being made free from the world,
through suffering and dying with Christ. (p. 302) And if a
demythologized resurrection or an existential authenticity
is primal for Bultmann, a real participation in the crucifixion is primary for Schweitzer, a dying in Christ that is a
dying from the world, and that death is a real and actual
death. Who could forget that Schweitzer was also a great
Bach scholar and organist? One can almost hear Bach's *St.
Matthew Passion* in Schweitzer's celebration of dying in
Christ, and if Luther was the greatest interpreter of Paul
since Augustine, Luther's theology of the cross is reborn in
Schweitzer's interpretation of Paul, but now justification
by faith is subordinated to redemption through being-in-
Christ. Indeed, Schweitzer insists that a Protestant justification by faith alone embodies a redemption from which
no ethic could logically be derived (p. 225).

Schweitzer's Paul knows that the world even now is in
process of apocalyptic transformation, a transformation
which is the immediate consequence of the crucifixion
and resurrection of Jesus, for Paul shares with Jesus an
apocalyptic faith and expectation: "The only difference is
the hour in the world-clock in the two cases" (p. 113). But
now Schweitzer breaks with his earlier interpretation of
Jesus:

> For the preaching of Jesus itself contains Christ-
> mysticism. It is simply not the fact that Jesus'
> preaching dealt with nothing but the nearness of
> the Kingdom of God and the ethic to be practised
> during the period of waiting; He also declared that
> in the fellowship with Him on which they had
> entered his followers had already the guarantee of

> future fellowship with the Son of Man. This Christ-
> mysticism He offers as a mystery. (p. 105)

The Bultmannian movement is determined to reverse that and every mystery, as an apocalyptic mystery becomes an eschatological-existential "Now," and *the salvation-occurrence is nowhere present except in the proclaiming, accosting, demanding, and promising word of preaching"* (p. 302). This categorical statement appears toward the conclusion of Bultmann's interpretation of Paul, a Paul who knew a uniqueness of God whose being is *"for us,"* and whose being is understood aright only when it is understood as being significant for human being, or *Dasein* (p. 229). So that for Bultmann Paul's theology is simultaneously anthropology, and so likewise is Paul's Christology anthropology, even if this is a soteriological anthropology. (p. 191) Yet nothing is so unclear in Bultmann as is his understanding of redemption, and at no other point is his method of demythologizing more important, for this is an understanding of redemption that is a deep reversal of both Gnostic and apocalyptic redemption. Nevertheless, Bultmann's understanding of a Pauline "flesh" clearly parallels both a Gnostic and an apocalyptic understanding of flesh, except for the all too significant fact that it centers upon a uniquely Pauline "I": "Therefore 'I' and 'I,' self and self, are at war with each other; i.e. to be innerly divided, or not to be at one with oneself; is the essence of human existence under sin" (p. 245). This is what Paul discovered as the universality of sin, a discovery that is the consequence of grace, for we may know God's grace only when we know God's wrath: "The will of God revealed to the Christian is identical with the demand of the Law" (p. 262). Yet the ultimate purpose of the Law is to lead humanity to death, and thereby "to let God appear as God"

(p. 267), for sin kills humanity by means of the command-ment by dangling before him the deceptive promise of producing life (Romans 7:11). But even this demand is only grace, and it was already grace that God gave the Law "for life" (Romans 7:10), and though this purpose was defeated by sin, it is still God's grace that the Law actually led to death, because it is by this way that we are led to God. Here a unity of the divine will is clear, but so, too, is the unity of human existence as it moves from the situation under Law to the situation under grace. No break takes place, no mystical or cosmic transformation, for a new human existence stands in historical continuity with the old (pp. 268–69).

This is a fundamental point at which Bultmann dis-tances his interpretation of Paul from both Gnosticism and apocalypticism, and he does so by a genuinely dialec-tical understanding of sin and grace, for even as each is inseparable from the other, each is truly itself only by way of the realization or actualization of the other. In this per-spective, we can see that it was Paul who created an un-derstanding of what the Christian most deeply knows as grace, and if that grace is an eschatologically redemptive grace, it is inseparable from an eschatological judgment. Bultmann reflects the influence of Luther and Augustine here, but he is even more deeply under the impact of Kierkegaard, who finally came to know the nothingness of *Angst*, or dread, as the consequence of a uniquely Chris-tian grace and forgiveness. Indeed, Bultmann's enormous hermeneutical strength in large measure derives from his theological power, and at no other point is contemporary New Testament interpretation so distant from Bultmann. Nor does Bultmann hesitate to confront Paul's deepest theological scandal—his declaration that for our sake God made Christ, who knew no sin, to be sin (2 Corinthians

5:21). Bultmann insists that this clause intends to express the paradoxical fact that God made the sinless Christ to be a sinner by submitting him to die on the cross as one accursed (Galatians 3:13). In his final publication, a commentary on second Corinthians,[8] Bultmann gravely weakens this interpretation by saying that God only regarded Christ as a sinner. In the *Theology of the New Testament*, he argues that just as the man of faith is not simply regarded by God as being righteous but really is righteous, so God made Christ *to be* sin so that we might become righteous (pp. 276–77). This is precisely what redemption is, and it is wholly by way of the grace of the crucifixion. And just as that crucifixion is a real death, our redemption, too, is a real state of righteousness, even if it defies all full understanding. Nevertheless, this is a redemption in which the ethical imperative not only does not contradict the indicative of justification, but results from it: "Cleanse out the old leaven that you may be fresh dough, as you really are unleavened" (1 Corinthians 5:7) (p. 332). So likewise, in his interpretation of faith as eschatological existence in the Gospel of John, he can insist upon *the dialectical relationship between indicative and imperative* (2:80). This is as close as Bultmann comes to giving us an understanding of redemption, and if he has effected a deep demythologizing of all Gnostic and apocalyptic mythology, such demythologizing is here inseparable from a uniquely Christian faith.

Nothing is more distinctive about Bultmann than his integral conjunction of New Testament scholarship and theological thinking, and if he is our only truly major New Testament scholar who is a full and genuine theologian, at no other point has his own impact been so enormous. Since his death, it has been the apocalyptic interpretation of the New Testament that has evolved most powerfully, yet it has been crippled by the fact that the Christian tradition itself has never evolved a genuine apocalyptic theology, or at least none that is manifestly theological. Above all there has been no apocalyptic understanding of God in theological thinking as such, and this is just the point at which New Testament theology has virtually collapsed, for the primal New Testament category of the Kingdom of God has yet to pass into theological thinking. Perhaps Ernst Kaesemann's *Commentary on Romans*[9] is as powerful a theological study of the New Testament as we have been given in the past generation, and Kaesemann does declare in the preface that the emphasis here will be upon what Paul meant theologically, and that he has sought systematic clarity (p. vi f.). However, in this anti-Bultmannian Bultmannian commentary, and one truly seeking and largely realizing an apocalyptic understanding of Paul, there is very little on either God or the Kingdom of God. When he does speak of God he speaks as a Bultmannian, as when he declares that justification means that God is there for us (p. 180) or that the new creature stands on "God for us and with us" (p. 136).

Nevertheless, Kaesemann does realize an apocalyptic understanding of the Pauline Christ, even if he remains a Bultmannian by knowing a Paul whose primary concern is for the eschatological miracle of "the humanization of man," which is prefigured by the crucified Christ and in which the coming of the new world takes place (p. 135). Kaesemann, too, is deeply Lutheran, accepting the theology of the cross as the key to Paul, and while justification here is the inauguration of the new creation, the center of Paul's theology is the justification of the ungodly, and "God alone fulfils what he demands" (p. 218). Kaesemann can be anti-Bultmannian in protesting against a reduction of Paul's theology to anthropology, and by insisting upon a fully and finally apocalyptic Paul, but it is highly questionable whether Kaesemann's understanding of justification fundamentally goes beyond Bultmann:

> For Paul real human beings, whether Jews or Gentiles, are ungodly, and are so also as pious persons. More than any other, Paul reflected deeply in his theology on what determined the words and deeds of Jesus according to Mark 2:17. Grace breaks into the sphere of wrath and the power of the gospel is shown in the disobedient. The deity of God displays itself in the fact that it uncovers the reality of human beings and thus opens the way to the humanity of man. Paul cannot let this be restricted to individuals, since God is for him the Creator of the world and not just the one who stands over against individuals. Hence salvation history in its universal breadth is linked to the doctrine of justification. (p. 317)

Another influential apocalyptic interpretation of Paul has come from the Calvinist perspective of J. C. Beker's *Paul the Apostle: The Triumph of God in Life and Thought*,[10] one which is truly anti-Bultmannian. Rather than affirming as Kaesemann does, that the crucified Lord has replaced the Torah, Beker insists that for Paul the crucified and risen Christ is the new Torah (p. 130). Despite its subtitle, his book contains little discussion of God and no attempt whatsoever to reach an apocalyptic understanding of God. Beker can go so far as to translate 1 Corinthians 15:28b as "that God may be everything to everyone" (p. 362). And while he understands the theme of the first epistle to the Corinthians to be the interrelationship of Spirit and body, he notes all too pointedly that the crucifixion is absent in Paul's celebration of the resurrection in the conclusion of

this epistle, despite the fact that it dominates the letter as
a whole. Beker is persuaded that Paul, more than any other
early theologian, opened the way to the doctrinal purity of
the gospel, and that he first did so through his reduction
of the gospel traditions to the gospel of "nothing except
Jesus Christ and him crucified" (1 Corinthians 2:2) (p. 131).
Hence, the absence of Jesus traditions is essential to Paul's
gospel. Not only is the resurrection of Christ the beginning of the new creation, but as a "bodily" resurrection it
signals the ontological transformation of the created order
in the Kingdom of God. Yet the death of Christ signifies
the "great reversal," because the judgment of the Torah on
Christ becomes instead the judgment of God in Christ on
the Torah (p. 186). Indeed, this is the triumph of God, and
it does not occur through the suffering of Christ, for unlike
Mark there is no passion of Christ in Paul, nor does the
cross need the confirmation of the resurrection, for it is in
the crucifixion and the crucifixion alone that there first
occurs the triumph of God. Here, Beker is radical, indeed—
so radical that perhaps this is a primary reason why so
little attention is given to God in the book as a whole.

Beker insists that Paul's focus on the apocalyptic dimension of the death of Christ is uniquely his own, for there
can be no doubt that the Antioch tradition views the death
of Christ in the context of his resurrection and the future
resurrection of the dead, a tradition that is present in 1
Corinthians 15. This misses the crucifixion itself as the
inauguration of the new age, as does every understanding
of the event of crucifixion as the event of resurrection, for
the crucifixion itself is the "great reversal," a cosmic and
apocalyptic reversal. Noting that Paul never speaks of Christ
as God, Beker refuses to speak of the Crucified God. But
perhaps he has done so nonetheless, by so forcefully calling
forth the crucifixion as the triumph of God.

> The theology of the cross is Paul's unique apoca-
> lyptic interpretation of the events of Jesus' death
> and resurrection, because it constitutes in most
> contexts the totality of meaning implicit in the
> Christ-event. The future age dawns in the cross,
> just as the old age comes to naught in it. Although
> the cross is primarily the dark side of God's vic-
> tory in the resurrection, its manifold meaning
> addresses the reality of Christian life not only as
> cruciform and weak but also as victorious in a
> cruciform mode, that is, as strong in its utter de-
> pendence on God's "transcendent power" (2 Cor-
> inthians 4:7) (p. 207)

But is it God's transcendent power that triumphs in the
death of Christ? And does it triumph by undergoing an
apocalyptic reversal of itself? Is it the transcendent glory
of God itself that is reversed in a truly and finally apocalyptic crucifixion? Beker never asks such questions, but
his own analysis makes them all but inevitable.

If the Pauline gospel is nothing else except Jesus Christ
and him crucified, is the Pauline Jesus nothing but the
crucified Jesus, a crucified Jesus who apocalyptically is all
in all? Just as Gnosticism can know a resurrected Jesus
who is all in all, did Paul himself in his deepest faith know
only a crucified Jesus? And was he thus inevitably impelled to ignore or transform the primitive Christian Jesus
traditions? How ironic that the Pauline epistles are the
first Christian writing, or the first along with early Q and
the earliest stratum of the Gospel of Thomas. For in all of
this writing no real attention is given to any Jesus save
Jesus the Savior. Yet in Paul alone is that Jesus only the
crucified Jesus. The resurrected Jesus of Paul is quite simply *pneuma* or Spirit, and if it is impossible to draw together a coherent Pauline account of Spirit, which is

certainly a major reason why the Corinthian correspondence is so extraordinarily difficult to interpret, it is equally difficult to find anything but a purely negative relationship between the Jesus "according to the Spirit" and the Jesus "according to the flesh." Certainly Paul's understanding of the Spirit fully sanctioned a Gnostic Paulinism. Marcion and the second-century Valentinian Gnostics were the first great interpreters of Paul, and their interpretations were inspired not only by the deutero-Pauline epistles but also by Paul's own language about Spirit.

If we see how deeply Pauline Marcionism and Valentiniasm are, we can detect a profoundly dialectical ground in Paul himself. Gnosticism can never know an "I" that is *sarx*, or "flesh" itself, and certainly not the "I" of *pneuma*. But Paul himself clearly and deeply embodied such an "I," and it is extraordinarily important that his letters have given us the first recorded presence of a doubled or self-alienated consciousness. Bultmann deeply grasped this self-division of consciousness as being the very essence of what Paul discovered as the universality of sin, and it is precisely the absence of such a doubling of consciousness which is the absence of an awareness of what Paul knew as sin. Innocence of any kind is impossible for the Pauline Christian, and although the Valentinians apparently transcended, or attempted to transcend, any awareness of the individual or self-conscious "I," that is an "I" which is a doubled "I," and hence an "I" which is deeply divided against itself. Now if that "I" could be understood to be a consequence of the crucifixion itself, and hence the consequence of a radically new and ultimate guilt, then a doubled self-consciousness would be the consequence of deep repression. Nietzsche and Freud discovered that very repression in the modern world, but it was known deeply in the ancient world by both Augustine and Paul.

Certainly Paul is the only known source of that deeply guilty consciousness that has so dominated Western culture, and at no other point is a Pauline impact so profound in the modern world. Psychoanalysis has been unable to resolve that guilt, just as it has never been truly transcended in the deepest expressions of our literature, so Paul is very much alive today, and perhaps most alive outside the Christian churches. Yet if that guilt is inseparable from what we have known as the center of consciousness, a center of consciousness which is the unique and individual "I," then such a center could be a witness to the crucifixion itself. For unless it is present in a few verses of Jeremiah or the Dead Sea Scrolls, it is surely absent in all the pre-Paul writing in the ancient world. At no other point was Paul so revolutionary as a writer, and if his writing is most deeply under the ultimate impact of the crucifixion, then the crucifixion surely is a dividing line in world history. All too significantly, it was Hegel who created our only full and genuine philosophy of history. The center of that philosophical history is the full advent of self-consciousness, which Hegel knew as occurring in the incarnation and being consummated in the crucifixion, a crucifixion that is the death of all abstract or alien Spirit and the full inauguration of an absolute self-consciousness. But a Hegelian self-consciousness realizes itself only by way of a deep, even absolute, self-negation. The kenotic movement of self-emptying or self-negation is the very center of Hegelian thinking, and that thinking is clearly a rebirth of Pauline thinking, and one which is vastly more powerful than anything which we have known as theological thinking.

But if historical scholarship can lead us to see that the Pauline Jesus is and only is the crucified Jesus, then surely this is the Jesus who is overwhelmingly powerful in the

modern world, and vastly more powerful than a crucified
Jesus was in the patristic and medieval Christian worlds.
The cross itself does not truly pass into Christian iconography until the end of the patristic age, and only very
gradually does it appear in medieval Christendom, not
decisively appearing until the fourteenth century, and not
becoming dominant until the very eve of the Reformation. And just as the birth of the modern world is the
birth of a full and even total self-consciousness, that self-
consciousness in all of its deeply imaginative expressions
is a profoundly divided and self-estranged consciousness. If
the birth of the modern world is a rebirth or renewal of
Paul, as it surely is in the Reformation, then that renewal
could be understood as a renewal of the crucifixion, and of
a uniquely Pauline crucifixion. When that crucifixion is
understood as an apocalyptic event, and not an apocalyptic
event but *the* apocalyptic event, then it is nothing less
than the ending of an old world, an "old aeon" which here
passes away, but only insofar as the crucifixion is an absolute event.

Yet the crucifixion could not be an absolute event if it
does not deeply and profoundly embody God, and if our
New Testament scholars have virtually ceased speaking
about God, perhaps their silence is a deep witness to the
crucifixion as the self-embodiment of God, a kenotic self-
emptying or self-negation, and precisely thereby a real and
actual apocalypse. How could a full apocalypse not be the
apocalypse of God? Did Gnosticism know such an apocalypse? And is that why Gnosticism is the most radical
movement in the ancient world? And if ancient Christian
orthodoxy evolved into an imperial and Constantinian
establishment, is that a consequence not only of a negation of Gnosticism, but also of a negation of Paul? Augustine is the only ancient orthodox theologian who was a

deeply Pauline theologian, but he is also the only ancient theologian who has been deeply reborn in the modern world, and even deeply reborn in our deepest modern thinking. Is that a rebirth of the Pauline Jesus? and therefore of the crucified Jesus? And even a Jesus who can be known only as the crucified Jesus? Surely no other Jesus is so powerful in our world, and if it is Paul who is the clearest source of that Jesus, then Paul may well be more powerfully present today than he has ever previously been in our history.

CHAPTER SIX

The Catholic Jesus:
Dante and Joyce

Nothing is a deeper mystery in Catholicism than the Christ who is its center. Not only is this Christ the fullness of humanity and deity at once, but his body is the very body of Catholicism itself, a sacred and natural body simultaneously, or a cosmic body that is nonetheless a magical body. The mystery of the Catholic Christ is inseparable from the Catholic Church itself, and if that Church is the most powerful religious world in history, its own advent is a truly revolutionary event, effecting a revolutionary transformation of its origins that occurred more rapidly and more comprehensively than any other historical revolution. Nothing in the history of religions even approaches the totality of the metamorphosis of primitive Christianity into Catholic Christianity. Yet this occurred in less than three generations, and did so in the context of an enormous diversity of early Christianity, ranging all the way from the genuine Gnosticism of the Thomas tradition to the deep apocalypticism of the Pauline and Markan traditions. No such comprehensive diversity and intense conflict is manifest in the advent of any other religious world, just as no other religious world has undergone such profound transformations in its historical evolution, with the possible exception of the transformation of Theravada into Mahayana Buddhism.

Catholicism may also well be unique in its progressive centering upon the Theotokos, or the Mother of God. She is minor, if not peripheral, in the gospels of Mathew and Luke, but by the fifth century of the Christian era, and at the Council of Ephesus in 431, not only is it dogmatically declared that the title of the holy Virgin Mary is Theotokos, but it is also declared that this is what the "exact faith" everywhere preaches.[1] These are the words of St. Cyril of Alexandria, a Doctor of the Church. Not only do they represent an orthodox victory over Nestorius's insistence that the exact title for Mary is *Christokos* and not *Theotokos*, but they also inevitably if only indirectly, signify a dogmatic victory of the primordial Goddess—a victory that is unique in the great world religions. Already images of the Great Goddess appear in Paleolithic and Neolithic icons, and they seemingly dominated that archaic religious world, but the advent of Israel was a profound challenge to the primordial Goddess. Archaeological evidence now suggests that the earliest pictorial portraits of Yahweh worship include "the asherah" as a consort of Yahweh,[2] but there can be no doubt that Israel's prophetic revolution shattered the domain of the Goddess in Israel, just as the Torah itself is a full and final negation of the Goddess. This negation is renewed in the earliest expressions of Christianity, with the all too significant exception of the Thomas tradition, which could know Jesus himself as the goddess Wisdom.

There is no graver historical problem in the history of religions than the origin of "The Mother of Wisdom," a goddess who is manifestly powerful throughout the ancient Near East. Her realm is both the cosmos and the whole of humanity, and she exists from the primordial beginning, but in a hidden form, so that she must be sought. The apocryphal Ecclesiasticus or The Wisdom of Jesus Son of Sirach can actually identify Wisdom with the Torah

(24.3ff.), and elsewhere Wisdom can appear as the "syzrgy" of God. But Wisdom is invariably a synchretistic deity in the Hellenistic world,[3] just as she is in the Book of Proverbs, but most powerfully synchretistic in Gnosticism itself. Yet nothing is more primal in Gnosticism than the fall of Wisdom or Sophia. This fall is perhaps the initial expression of what Jonas understands as the "devolution" of the Gnostic Godhead, and the Apocryphon of John can actually know Sophia as the Mother of Ialtabaoth or Satan (9:25:10:26). There is also a Gnostic Trinity, composed of the Father, the Mother, and the Son, which are progressive emanations of the Godhead, as in the Gospel of the Egyptians. A fourth-century orthodox theologian, Marcellus of Ancyra, can even assert that Valentinus was the first to devise the notion of three subsistent hypostases of the Godhead, the three persons of the Father, the Son, and the Holy Spirit.[4] According to Irenaeus, Valentinus's disciple, Ptolemy, could know the suffering of Sophia as the passion of the crucifixion,[5] a passion reversing the original fall of Sophia, and so it is that the identity riddles in "Thunder, Perfect Mind" can unveil Sophia as a *coincidentia oppositorum*:

> For it is I who am the first; and the last.
> It is I who am the revered; and the despised.
> It is I who am the harlot; and the holy.
> It is I who am the wife; and the virgin.
> It is I who am the mother; and the daughter.[6]

Clearly the second century of the Christian era is when the greatest conflict between orthodoxy and Gnosticism occurred, but this was the era in which the Catholic theology of Our Lady was truly born, and perhaps born in Irenaeus's understanding of Mary as the new Eve, wherein the knot of Eve's disobedience was untied by Mary's obedience.[7] This may well be the original seed of the dogma of the Theotokos, and little more than a century later, Eusebius of Caeserea, could know the very word *Theotokos* as the touchstone of orthodoxy,[8] just as only a little latter St. Gregory of Nazianzus could declare that anyone who does not believe Mary to be Theotokos is an atheist.[9] Yet before the tenth century there is no record of theological statements affirming Mary's role in redemption, and not until the thirteenth century does the idea of a partnership between Jesus and Mary arise. But then there is an enormous outburst of the theology of the Mother of God, culminating in the fourteenth century in Byzantium in Gregory Palamas, who could declare: "No divine gifts can reach either angels or men, save through her mediation . . . so every movement towards God, every impulse towards good coming from him is unrealizable save through the mediation of the Virgin."[10] Yet perhaps the symbol of Mary Mediatress is first decisively born in the West, and born even in one of the great "heretics" of the West, Peter Abelard, who could affirm that Mary is "our Mediatress to the Son as he is to the Father."[11]

Little as we may actually know about Abelard's theology of the Mother of God, he lived and thought in the very eve of the Gothic revolution of Western Christianity, one creating a new Catholicism as distant from the patristic world as it is from the modern world, and whose greatest and most revolutionary visionary was Dante Alighieri. If we conceive the Gothic world as a historical world that fully and integrally unites time and Eternity, then nowhere is that world so luminously present as it is in Dante's *Commedia*. The full and actual reality of time is not only negated and transcended in Eternity, but is also preserved as time itself, even if this is a new time that is an apocalyptic time, but a real and actual apocalyptic time. The Gothic revolution transformed an entire millennium of

Christian history, and transformed it by discovering the transcendence of Eternity in the actuality of time itself, as time once again becomes an apocalyptic time, a time in which Eternity is here and now. Now time itself is simultaneously an earthly and chronological time and a sacred and eternal time, a simultaneity revealed in the very chronology of the *Commedia*. The epic action of the *Commedia* occurs during Eastertide in the year 1300 and lasts just a week, from the night of Maundy Thursday, when Dante finds himself astray in the Dark Wood, until noon on the Wednesday after Easter, when Dante is transfigured in Heaven. The period of Dante's descent into Hell repeats and renews the time of Christ's death and burial, just as his journey through Purgatory renews and repeats the time of Christ's entombment and descent into Hell, and his entrance into Paradise coincides with the dawn of Easter Sunday. A Pauline and early Christian participation even now in the Crucifixion and the Resurrection of Christ is now fully realized in the temporal reality of this epic history, in the spring of the year 1300, and in the life and experience of its epic hero, Dante Alighieri, when he was the very age that was the established age of the crucified and resurrected Christ.

Yet nothing is more theologically revealing of the *Commedia* than the virtual absence of the temporal, the human, and the historical Christ. His name cannot be spoken in Hell, and accordingly is absent from the *Inferno*, and it is remarkable that in the thirty-nine times in which the name of Christ is employed in the *Commedia*, there is never a reference to the human or historical Jesus. Instead there are invocations and celebrations of the Son of God who is Lord, Emperor, Light, Word, Wisdom, and Power. While Christ is our bliss and our redeemer, bridegroom of poverty and the church, he is so always as the true God, the God of pure and absolute transcendence. The one actual

reference to the crucified God speaks not of Christ but of
"Jove supreme" (*Purgatorio* VI, 118), and even the single
reference to the "breast of our Pelican" (*Paradiso* XXV,
113) is simply a way of identifying Mary as being closest
to Christ. True, the story of Christ is told through the
story of St. Francis (*Paradiso* XI), but it is significant that
when Dante tells this story, he gives no images or in-
sights of his own, but simply transcribes into verse a few
passages from St. Bonaventura's *Legend of the Blessed
Francis.* The simple truth is that the human Christ is not
and cannot be present in the *Commedia* because Dante
knows and celebrates Christ only as the absolutely transcendent God, a God who cannot actually become incarnate as God, and certainly cannot suffer and die as God.
At this point and others, Dante is seemingly a genuine
Thomist. But he knows a transcendence of Christ that is
far more radical than Aquinas knew, just as he knows an
intimate and interior grace that defies all scholastic
understanding.

Christ's person appears at only a single point in the
Commedia—in canto XXIII of the *Paradiso*, when Dante
led by Beatrice sees the eighth heaven of the fixed stars
and the Church Triumphant. Then, for but an instant, he
sees Christ as the "One Sun" that enlightens all the stars,
a clear and shining "Substance" so bright that even his
now transfigured eyes cannot bear it. Beatrice reveals to
Dante that this Light that has overcome him is a power
from which there is no defense, then Dante's soul is carried wholly away from itself, and Beatrice summons him
for the first time to open his eyes and look at her as she
is. Yet even when Dante now enters the beatific vision, he
cannot actually see Christ, but only Beatrice. Although his
fragmentary glimpse of an absolutely exalted Christ might
well have made possible his full vision of Beatrice, it is,

indeed, Dante's vision of Beatrice that realizes his full and actual entry into Eternity. Then a transfigured cosmos and time are present only in Beatrice—the Beatrice who had initially summoned Virgil to rescue Dante from the Dark Wood, and who appears in glory at the end of the *Purgatorio* to replace a now disappeared Virgil as Dante's guide and shepherd in Paradise. This is the same Beatrice whom Dante had met when she was a young Florentine girl in 1274, and who had died in 1290, inspiring Dante's *La Vita Nuova*, in which Dante first identifies Beatrice as the celestial light of heaven. If only in vision, Beatrice initiated Dante into a truly individual experience of Eternity, thereby releasing an anagogical vision that is uniquely Dante's own. That mystical experience finally made possible a new language of Beatrician love, arising from a unique historical world, and from a truly singular Beatrice, and a Beatrice who preserves such an individuality even in her voice and epiphany in Heaven. For Dante, Beatrice was the very embodiment of grace. Indeed, she was the instrument, and the sole actual instrument of redeeming grace. Consequently, for the epic hero and the creator of the *Commedia*, Beatrice is the sole full image, and the only intimate and interior presence, of the incarnate Christ, of that Christ in whom time and Eternity are one.

Of course, after his death Dante was condemned by the Pope himself as a heretic. The papacy condemned him for his negation of the temporal authority and status of the Catholic Church, but Dante's far deeper heresy was the identification of Beatrice with the incarnate Christ. This made possible the imaginative revolution of the *Commedia*, but it is openly opposed to the established dogma of the Church, and is a universe removed from the *Summa Theologica*. Yet medieval Christianity did not even notice such ultimate heresy, and could not notice it, for the birth of the Gothic world occurred with a universal epiphany of the Mother of God as the immanent source of redemptive grace. The Gothic cathedrals themselves were erected as sanctuaries and embodiments of the divine Mother, and for the first time in Christian history worship and devotion were far more fully and more ecstatically directed to the Mother of God than to the Son of God, and the annunciation replaced the nativity as the primary icon in Christian art, a transformation that is fulfilled in the *Commedia*. At no other point is a resurrection of the ancient world more fully present in the Gothic world. But this is not a rebirth of an archaic or Oriental Goddess, it is rather a rebirth of the Greek Goddess, and not the awesome and numinous Goddess of Euripides, but rather the intimately gracious Goddess of the highest moments of Greek sculpture.[12] Of course, there is little more than a hint of such a figure in the New Testament. Even if the Mother of God is present as the personified Wisdom of the Book of Proverbs, and perhaps as the Bride in the Song of Songs, she is never present as a full and actual Goddess. But who could doubt that the Queen of Heaven who undergoes an ecstatic epiphany in the highest heaven of the *Paradiso* is the Great Goddess?

After entering the beatific vision, Dante has three visions of the eternal Virgin, and in the last vision he actually sees the face that most resembles Christ, and only its radiance now grants Dante the power to look upon Christ (XXXII, 86). The final canto of the *Paradiso* opens with a prayer of St. Bernard of Clairvaux to the Virgin Mother, a prayer that declares:

> "Virgin Mother, daughter of thy Son,
> humble and exalted more than any creature,
> fixed goal of the eternal counsel, thou art she

who didst so enoble human nature that its
Maker did not disdain to become its creature.[13]

The Italian of the last clause has a sound and meaning that
cannot be reproduced in translation—*che 'l suo fattore
disdegno di farsi sua fattura*—but it is nevertheless wholly
clear that it is the Mother of God who has transformed
humanity so as to make possible the Incarnation. Thus
the real work of redemption occurs in the womb of Mary
rather than in the crucifixion, effected by a Mother of
God who is not simply coredemptress but here is
Mediatrix Redemptrix. Thereby Dante not only fully
anticipated a much later Mariology, but also unveiled one
of the deepest grounds of the Gothic revolution itself,
which is nothing less than the resurrection of a truly
primordial world.

The *Commedia* is the first Christian writing and vision
to fully integrate a Classical history and mythology with
the Christian world. Although it is based upon the theological revolution of Aquinas, which truly integrated "nature" and grace, it goes far beyond Aquinas by not only
integrating but by actually uniting history and revelation,
which here and only here in the Christian world is a full
and actual integration of cosmos, consciousness, history
and revelation, as a new totality is unveiled whereby and
wherein a primordial and an apocalyptic totality are one.
Nowhere in the Gothic world is such an integration more
manifestly present than in a truly new and even apocalyptic epiphany of the Mother of God, that Great Goddess
who for Dante is truly embodied in Beatrice, a Beatrice
who is that actual and individual one who embodies the
primordial Mother's compassion for Dante, and who is
the one and only way of salvation for the first epic hero of
the Christian world. Only in Beatrice is incarnate deity

present for this epic hero, and while the eternal light of Beatrice may ultimately be the light of the Son or "Sun," it is humanly or actually seeable only in an incarnation of the Mother of God. Accordingly, the only deity that even a transfigured and beatified Dante can actually see is the Goddess, first present in the Beatrice whom Dante can finally and fully see, and then present in the Virgin, whom Dante can now see even if he cannot actually see Christ.

Yet a beatified Dante does, indeed, see Christ by seeing the Mother of God. This is the only vision of God that is possible in even the highest heaven of the Empyrean, just as this is precisely that highest Gothic anagogic vision that realizes a full and actual union of time and Eternity, a truly apocalyptic vision, and one unveiling the glory and the compassion of the Godhead itself. But that Godhead is not simply an infinitely distant or wholly other transcendence, for the *Commedia* culminates in a visionary voyage into the deepest depths of the "Infinite Goodness," depths wherein an interiorly resurrected Dante sees the scattered limbs or leaves of the universe itself bound by love "in one single body" (*Paradiso* XXXIII, 86). Such a vision is far distant from any scholastic theological understanding, just as it is vastly distant from the whole world of ancient or patristic Christianity, but this is a world which is wholly alien to a Beatrician love and compassion. Beatrice herself is first unveiled in canto XXXI of the *Purgatorio*: this is the most intimate canto of the *Commedia*, and the only one in which Dante records his own name. Here, Beatrice discloses to Dante that never did either nature or art set before him beauty so great as is present in her body, and while that body has now crumbled into dust, the ultimate desire it released in Dante is finally directed to a love of that goodness beyond which there is nothing to be longed for. Above all it is in Beatrice that a *quia* or "thatness" is actual and manifest, a *quia* that is the very heart of the real as real, and that is graciously given to us even in the absence of a total understanding that would have precluded the necessity of the Incarnation (*Purgatorio* III, 37). Finally, this *quia* is unspeakable, but it is indubitably real as a fully present and intimate actuality, an actuality which is the ground of full vision, and a reality which is actual here and now.

In Virgil's discourse on love in canto 18 of the *Purgatorio*, love is unveiled as the very center of the creation. Love is now called forth even in the sensory act of perception, for an actual and individual perception unfolds within us an interior reality, and our interior turning to that reality is the movement of love, a response to a creation that is finally "isness" and love at once. This is the *quia* which is manifest in Dante's Beatrice, and its actuality is an embodiment of a glorious beauty that is the love that moves the sun and the stars and that is latently present in every act of perception. This integration of nature and grace revolutionizes Dante's Thomistic ground, by calling forth an apocalyptic totality that is alien both to Aquinas and to every scholastic thinker, and most alien precisely as a totally present totality. Not insignificantly, Joachim of Fiore, who was the first Catholic apocalyptic theologian, and the source of the deepest heresies in the medieval world, if not in our world as well, appears as a redeemed and shining prophet in the *Paradiso* (XII, 140), and ironically appears with St. Bonaventura, the Franciscan minister general who successfully opposed the Franciscan Spirituals who were so deeply inspired by Joachim. Yet we know that Dante himself was a deeply apocalyptic believer, as fully manifest in *De Monarchia*, which was condemned to the flames and placed on the Index by Pope John the Twelfth in the year of Meister Eckhart's condemnation, 1329. *De Monarchia* was written between 1309 and 1313, a crucial period in Dante's own transformation as an artist and visionary, and it was immediately followed by the beginning of the composition of the *Commedia*. At that time Dante was virtually obsessed by a radical messianic vision, in which he believed that the Emperor Henry VII was the promised Messiah, and this is the context in which Dante looks upon a new Christian Empire as an ultimate apocalyptic goal, and one establishing a true equality between the Empire and the Catholic Church. With the death of Henry VII in 1313 this hope perished, and out of Dante's profound disenchantment gradually issued forth the creation of the *Commedia*.

The *Commedia* is a far more deeply apocalyptic work than *De Monarchia*. It, too, renews an original Christian apocalyptic vision, one negated by the very triumph of the original Catholic Church. But now and for the first time a full Catholic vision is an apocalyptic vision, and hence it is inevitably heretical and orthodox at once. So, too, is Dante's Christ orthodox and heretical simultaneously, and if this is a Christ in whom the human Jesus has wholly disappeared, it is precisely that disappearance that makes possible a total and apocalyptic epiphany of the Mother of God. Yet if the Mother of God is fully incarnate in Dante's Beatrice, this and this alone here makes possible an apocalyptic epiphany of the cosmos itself, a universe that is bound by love to the deepest depths of the Godhead, so that the very act of perception itself is a realization of love, and of that love that is the very center both of the cosmos and of Godhead itself. A radically new vision is here at hand, and one in which deity, world, and humanity are fully integrated and united. If this is our only fully unified Christian vision, it is so only by way of the disappearance of Jesus, or the disappearance of a Jesus who is not fully embodied in the cosmic and primordial body of the Mother of God.

Dante not only created the Christian epic, or the Christian epic as epic poetry; he thereby created the Christian epic hero, a hero who is simultaneously Dante himself and a universal humanity, and a hero embodying the new self-consciousness that dawns with the very advent of Christianity. But now, and for the first time, the fullness and actuality of self-consciousness passes into poetic language itself, thereby effecting a revolutionary transformation of Western poetry, a transformation paralleling Giotto's transformation of Western painting. *The Inferno* is the first full poetic embodiment of self-consciousness, and it is an embodiment realizing a truly new human being. This is a human being it is true portrayed by Giotto, and portrayed as a unique and individual human being, but now that human being speaks for the first time, and speaks through the "*io sol uno*," the "I myself alone" of Dante (*Inferno* II, 3). This uniquely individual and interior subject is the very center of the Christian world. It only gradually realizes itself in Western history, first becoming a conceptual and interior subject in Augustine's theological thinking, and then bursting forth in the Gothic revolution, and above all so in Dante, a revolution which is the very advent of what we know as the modern world.

If ours is the time of the ending of that world, that, too, was anticipated by Dante, just as Dante's epic and apocalyptic world is reborn in the epic and apocalyptic world of James Joyce. Certainly only Dante is Joyce's full precursor, and just as Dante is the greatest visionary of a fully historical Catholicism, Joyce is the greatest visionary of the dark underground of Catholicism, an underground embodying a pure transgression, but one which is nevertheless a profoundly Catholic transgression, and a transgression which would be wholly unreal apart from its deep Catholic ground. But nothing could be realer than Joyce's epic writing, a writing which is not only prose and poetry at once, but voice and writing or scripture at once, as our epic poetry culminates in a universal voice, and a universal voice that is interior and exterior or human and cosmic simultaneously. Now a primordial world that was first epically resurrected in the *Commedia* passes into a purely immediate actuality, an actuality which is the brute immediacy of our common and everyday life. Never before had such an actuality undergone a full metamorphosis into writing and text, just as never before was a text created that is antitext, or whose textual embodiment disembodies writing or scripture itself. This occurs, of course, in *Finnegans Wake*, but the *Wake* is not only the full resolution of Joyce's writing, but the culmination of our Western literature as well, a culmination that is ending or apocalypse itself.

That interior and individual subject that is so fully embodied in Dante's writing now reverses itself, a reversal which is an apocalyptic reversal, and one thereby ending that subject itself. But that subject ends only in a full and final epiphany of its opposite, an epiphany which is an epiphany of Dante's primordial and apocalyptic totality, but now a totality that is an absolutely prosaic and profane totality, and thereby a reversal of Dante's sacred universe. Nevertheless, Joyce's epic vision is profoundly Catholic. Not only does a Catholic heresy now become a total heresy, and a total blasphemy as well, but an epic realizes itself through a uniquely Catholic liturgy, thereby realizing once again a total epiphany of the uniquely Catholic Mother of God. Only in *Finnegans Wake* does a liturgical language and action become fully embodied in writing and text. Even if this is a reverse embodiment, and hence a reversal of the Roman rite, it nevertheless is a fully liturgical embodiment, and inevitably has a fully ritual effect upon its reader or hearer. This is the most manifest source of the sheer power of this work, which inevitably draws us into its continually enacted liturgical sacrifice, and if this is once again a sacrifice of a uniquely Catholic Host, it has all the power of liturgical sacrifice, a power that was a grounding center of our history for hundreds of thousands of years.

Critical analysis has now fully established the incredibly intricate and organic structure of *Ulysses*, a structure whose only real historical precedent is the *Commedia*, but nonetheless a structure whose very form and mode conjoins and unites cosmos and chaos, so that this epic realization of a fully modern cosmic order is simultaneously and necessarily an apocalyptic epiphany of a long hidden but original primordial abyss. Now that abyss fully passes into language and text, and does so more comprehensively and more finally than ever previously in the West, even if this all-too-modern epic is in full continuity with the Christian epic from Dante through Blake. But now a new language is truly born, though it is in full continuity with its past, as is so marvelously manifest in episode 14, which reenacts the history of English prose from its beginnings to modern slang. Yet that very history irrefutably demonstrates the newness of the language now at hand, a language in which exterior and interior are indistinguishable from one another, in which subject as subject is everywhere and everyone, and in which object is totally exterior and factually overwhelming even while being indistinguishable from its speaker or subject. If a uniquely modern language is a language of chaos, or a language in which cosmos and chaos become one, it is here a language recovering a primal rite or ritual that had been dissolved or erased by the very evolution of language in the West. So it is that Joyce's recovery of liturgical language is inevitably a renewal of a primordial abyss, one that he could know as the deepest ground of the Catholic Church, as Stephen declares in *Ulysses*:

> Fatherhood, in the sense of conscious begetting, is unknown to man. It is a mystical estate, an apostolic succession, from only begetter to only begotten. On that mystery and not on the madonna which the cunning Italian intellect flung to the mob of Europe the church is founded, like the world, macro- and microcosm, upon the void.[14]

Certainly a continual enactment of a primordial abyss or void becomes progressively ever more dominant in Joyce's work, until it triumphs in *Finnegans Wake*. But that enactment is inseparable from an ever fuller calling forth of a purely ritual language that disenacts or disembodies a mythical language, as we can see by the very role of Jesus in both *Ulysses* and *Finnegans Wake*. At the conclusion of the Proteus episode of *Ulysses*, which initiates Stephen hero into his new epic role, an initiation ritually occurs by way of a passage through death, a death now making manifest a cosmic incarnation, an incarnation in which "God becomes man becomes fish . . . " But this "fish" is Christ as a purely ritual victim, and as such a victim wholly dissociated from any mythical form of Christ, a victim who is pure victim as such and no more, and hence by necessity a nameless or anonymous Christ.

> Come. I thirst. Clouding over. No black clouds anywhere, are there? Thunderstorm. Allbright he falls, proud lightning of the intellect, *Lucifer, dico, qui nescit occasum*. No. My cockle hat and staff and

his may sandal shoon. The evening lands. Evening
will find itself. (p. 50)

Christ here and now becomes indistinguishable from that
Lucifer who falls and yet knows no fall. Joyce's Latin phrase
is taken from a phrase in the Catholic liturgy for Holy
Saturday, the Easter Vigil, and the Joyce who publicly and
privately scorned Catholicism was the Joyce who, although
habitually a late riser, never failed throughout his life to
get up about five o'clock in all weathers to attend the early
morning mass on Holy Thursday and Good Friday.[15]
   The Son of God appears dogmatically in *Ulysses* only in
a purely heretical form, and most clearly so in Sabellian
Trinitarianism: "Sabellius, the African, the subtlest her-
esiarch of all the beasts of the field, held that the Father
was Himself His own Son" (p. 208). This is the Father who
thereby is invisible as Father, but this invisibility creates
the mystery upon which the Catholic Church is founded,
a mystery that is manifestly present only in the Latin liturgy. Now that mystery is wholly dissociated from Catholic theology, thereby ritual itself is dissociated from myth,
and a primal rite is called forth that is mythically anonymous or nameless. Accordingly, the Catholic God is now
only a noise or a voice in the street (pp. 34, 186), even if
He is thereby a "Hangman God" who is doubtless all in all
in all of us (p. 213). But this does make possible a new or
perhaps renewed prayer to: "Our father who art not in
heaven" (p. 227), the very prayer that is here prayed to
prepare the way for the apocalyptic return of Elijah, thereby
initiating an apocalypse that is the "new Bloomsusalem"
(p. 484). Leopold Bloom is the primary epic hero in *Ulysses*,
that perfectly ordinary man who is extraordinary only in
his ordinariness, but who is factually and bodily present in

this epic as no epic hero has been before. Moreover, Bloom is a ritual victim throughout the epic, and if this openly occurs only in the Circe episode, he is nonetheless a foil for the most inhuman speech and action throughout the epic, and not simply because of his Jewish origin and loyalty, but rather because his simple but deep humanity is simultaneously the center of this epic even as it is its most alien periphery or boundary.

Here is a passion story that is a prosaic story, or a prosaic enactment of the passion. Bloom is the most open embodiment of Jesus in *Ulysses*, and this is one which is wholly dissociated from the Catholic Christ, except insofar as that Christ is a purely ritual victim. Christianity has always most deeply known Jesus as a *coincidentia oppositorum*, an absolutely paradoxical union of time and eternity and of the finite and the infinite. But its Catholic and orthodox christologies have never truly realized such a union, invariably either isolating the humanity and deity of Christ or knowing his humanity only as a docetic appearance. Such docetism finally ends in Joyce's epic enactments, as here a pure orthodoxy can only be realized as pure heresy, just as a uniquely Western order can now be realized only through chaos itself. An intrinsic source of the power of *Ulysses* is its full conjunction of a comprehensive and total structure and order, an order renewing in a new world the total order and universe of the *Commedia*, with a wholly spontaneous and free movement and speech that are every bit as arbitrary and senseless as are the most actual moments of our lives. Thereby the conjunction and coinherence of cosmos and chaos become actual and real, and finally real in the total presence of a *coincidentia oppositorum*, a *coincidentia* of total opposites, which never before had passed into scripture or text in such a pure form. Although each episode of this epic is a fully individual organism with its own structure and language, each is simultaneously an integral organic component of the epic as a whole, for each episode of *Ulysses* is its own microscopic center even while being inseparable from a macroscopic whole. Yet the comprehensive movement of the epic, and of its seemingly diverse and isolated episodes, is wholly free and spontaneous, thereby embodying a truly new union of freedom and necessity, wherein an individual freedom and self-consciousness are not only inseparable but indistinguishable from a cosmic order and necessity.

Just as modern physics could discover a random and arbitrary microscopic energy and movement that nevertheless embody a total and comprehensive order transcending any order known in our past, so likewise Joyce's epics discover and embody a fully arbitrary and random linguistic and human energy and movement that are simultaneously a cosmic and an organic order. Accordingly, it is not odd to discover a ritual order and movement in *Ulysses*, even if this is realized in a wholly profane, historical, and prosaic world. Indeed, the full conjunction of the archaic and the modern is a primary and primordial source of the authority and the power of *Ulysses*. Now the world itself becomes the sanctuary where this epic and linguistic movement occurs, and a sanctuary making possible a new center and victim, a victim who is an absolutely ordinary human being. Only such a prosaic and fully concrete and factual ritual victim could break down all barriers between the altar and the world, or between rite and actuality, or between a ritual and a total presence. Then the Eucharist becomes not only a cosmic but also a historical mass, a mass enacted in our history and world, and enacted at the very center of its brute facticity and actuality. This is the mass that undergoes a universal realization in *Finnegans*

Wake, and the *Wake* is inseparable from *Ulysses,* even as Blake's *Jerusalem* is inseparable from his *Milton.*

Now that it has been well established that it is the final monologue of Molly and the dream language and action of the Circe episode which opened the way to the night or "not" language of *Finnegans Wake,* it is essential to recognize not simply the continuity between *Ulysses* and *Finnegans Wake,* but also their deep unity, and a unity which is fully manifest in their epic action, which is finally a cosmic sacrifice or mass. That mass begins in the *Wake* with the original fall of Satan on its first page. But this Satan is the Creator, a uniquely modern epiphany of the Creator who is now a cosmic sacrificial Host, and it is the cosmic and historical sacrifice of this Host which is continually reenacted throughout the text of *Finnegans Wake.* That is precisely why this text is a liturgical text, a liturgical text calling forth the deepest blasphemy that has ever been recorded, a blasphemy inevitably and necessarily called forth by that ultimate transgression that occurs here. The very first pages of the *Wake* to be written, pages 380–82, eventually became the conclusion of book II, chapter iii, which is both the central or axial chapter of the *Wake* and also the most difficult and complex section of this dream or night epic. Now the cosmic mass is a dream mass, but it is a Eucharist nonetheless, and a Eucharistic feast, culminating in the cosmic consumption of Earwicker or H.C.E., who is Leopold Bloom reborn as "Here Comes Everybody." But the virtually literal center of the earliest writing in the *Wake* is a divine acceptance of sacrificial death—*I've a terrible errible lot todue todie todue tooterrible day*—an ultimate death that is not only the center of a historically cosmic Holy Week, but that occurs again and again throughout the epic. The universal humanity

of the *Wake* is both a legendary Ireland and a contemporary Dublin pub, and H.C.E. is both a local innkeeper and
the most glorious divine and heroic king of our archaic
past. Both the action and the speech of the *Wake* are
divine and human simultaneously, a simultaneity which
is also present in a mystery play or drama that is the
universal history of humanity. Although everything is the
same in this eternal recurrence or return, it is the "same
anew" (215.23), and the "mystery repeats itself todate"
(294.28).

The Dublin "ostman" or Norseman, H. C. Earwicker, is
both "Haar Faagher" and the ancient Celtic hero, Finn
MacCool, but he is also Yggdrasil or the cosmic Tree, which
in the Eddas symbolizes the universe, a universe that goes
on trial as the "Festy King" in chapter three of Book II.
The fall, condemnation, and crucifixion of H.C.E. is the
dominant epic action of the *Wake*, and just as the liturgical acts and action of the mass culminate in communion,
so fall and death culminate in a festival or orgiastic communion in this apocalyptic epic. This communion issues
in a blasphemy, even a scatological blasphemy, that undergoes a constant ritual repetition in the text. But lying at
the center of this epic, even as the breaking of the Host
lies at the center of the mass, is the execution or crucifixion of "Haar Faagher," which becomes most dramatic and
most scatological in the television skit by the comics Butt
and Taff of "How Buckley Shot the Russian General." This
occurs in the axial chapter of the *Wake*, and it culminates
in the tavern orgy that is the cosmic repetition of an Easter that is Good Friday, a resurrection that is an ecstatic
consumption of the crucified Body of God. But this cosmic
Easter is possible only as a consequence of the breaking of
the Host:

How Buccleuch shocked the rosing girnirilles. A
ballet of Gasty Power. A hov and az and off like a
gow! And don't live out the sad of tearfs, paddya-
whick! Not offgot affsang is you, buthbach? Ath
yetheredayth noch endeth hay? Vaersegood! Buckle
to! (346.20)

After the announcement of this primal event, H.C.E. is
himself accused of the primordial crime or fall, whereupon
he pleads guilty (363.20), and then identifies himself with
his own executioner: " . . . I am, I like to think, by their
sacreligion of daimond cap daimond, confessedly in my
baron gentilhomme to the manhor bourne til ladiest day
as panthoposopher, to have splet for groont a peer of bel-
lows like Bacchulus shakes a rousing guttural at any old
cerpaintime by peaching (allsole we are not amusical) the
warry warst against myself in the defile as a libererretter
sebaiscopal . . ." (365.3–10)

Yet this death of God is the self-sacrifice of God, a sacrifice renewing both primordial sacrifice and the Crucifixion itself. Not only is the executed the executioner, but
the condemned one is the eternal Judge, and nothing whatsoever distinguishes guilt and condemnation or fall and
execution, because Victim and Judge and Host and Creator
are one. So it is the Sabellian Trinitarianism of *Ulysses*
now passes into a cosmic Trinitarianism, a Trinitarianism
in which the Creator is the sacrificial Victim, and is so
precisely as Creator, or precisely as the uniquely Christian
God, or that God who in Christ is the atoning and sacrificial Victim. Now this crucifixion is "Fenegans Wick," as
this "kinn of all Fenns" passes into and is consumed as a
"Fisht" (376.34), and an "easter greeding" occurs when we
hear the solemn tones of the Sanctus: "Angus! Angus!
Angus!":

Laying the cloth, to fore of them. And thanking the
fish, in core of them. To pass the grace for Gard
sake! Ahmohn. Mr. Justician Mathews and Mr.
Justician Marks and Mr. Justician Luk de Luk and
Mr. Justician Johnson-Johnson. And the aaskart, see,
behind! Help, help, hurray! Allsup, allsop! Four
ghools to nail! Cut it down mates, look slippy!
They've got a dathe with a swimminpull. Dang!
Ding! Dong! Dung! Dinnin. Isn't it great he is sway-
ing above us for his good and ours. Fly your bal-
loons, dannies, and dennises! Her's doorknobs dead!
And Annie Delap is free. Ones more. We could ate
you, par Buccas, and imbabe through you,
reassuranced in the wild lac of gotliness. One fledge,
one brood till hulm culms evurdyburdy. Huh the
throman! Huh the traidor. Huh the truh. (377.29–
378.6)

Of course, A.L.P. or Anna Livia Plurabelle is also the
epic hero or heroine of the *Wake*, and Book One closes
with the passage of A.L.P. into "Night now!"—an A.L.P.
who is the "same anew," Anna was, Livia is, Plurabelle's
to be—and an A.L.P. who is inseparable from *Hircus Civis
Eblanensis!*, the goat citizen or scapegoat of Dublin and
the world. This is the H.C.E. who repeatedly falls and is
pursued and condemned throughout Book One, and then
is crucified at the end of Book Two, a crucifixion which is
reenacted as creation in Book Three, which closes with
H.C.E. and A.L.P. fallen into a fatal sleep: "O, foetal sleep!
Ah, fatal slip! the one loved, the other left, the bride of
pride leased to the stranger!" (563.10). Not only is this
sleep a renewal of the conclusion of *Ulysses*, but it is also
a renewal of Dante's and Virgil's descent into Hell, and
once again it culminates in an Easter resurrection, which
is the apocalyptic resurrection of Book Four. Dante's

Beatrice is present once again in Anna Livia Plurabelle, and the Catholic Mother of God now undergoes her ultimate epiphany, an epiphany ecclesiastically sanctioned by the proclamation of the dogma of the Immaculate Conception by Pius IX in 1854 and by the proclamation of the dogma of Mary's bodily ascension into Heaven by Pius XII in 1950, dogmas going beyond the glorification of the Mother of God in Eastern Orthodoxy, just as they went beyond even their medieval roots. Yet H.C.E. never openly or manifestly appears in Book Four, for this is the time of the first and last "rittlerrattle of the anniverse" or riddle of the universe "when is a name nought a name whenas it is a" (607.11). This is that unique and apocalyptic time when darkness is light and pure darkness is pure light. Indeed, this is the Day of Resurrection, a day when East and West meet in darkness, but it is thereby "Adya" or today.

The Easter celebration of Book Four opens with the Sanctus that is the preface to the great prayer of consecration in the canon of the mass—"Sandhyas! Sandhyas! Sandhyas!"—now chanted in Sanskrit, because East and West are now one. An elusive motif of the *Wake* is now decoded. This is the Augustinian phrase, "securus judicat orbis terrarum," that converted John Henry Newman. This phrase, in various transpositions, appears again and again in the *Wake*, and not only is it testimony to Joyce's conviction that Newman is the greatest prose stylist in the English language, but it offers yet another Catholic ground of Joyce's vision, and one that is not fully called forth theologically until the creation of this epic. For this is the theological ground that states both the nature and the identity of Catholic authority: the judgment of the whole world cannot be wrong. But now *securus judicat* becomes *securest jubilends* (593.13), as an external and exterior authority passes into a universal *missa jubilaea*,[16] a cosmic and apocalyptic mass that is not only the enactment of a universal sacrifice, but a universal sacrifice that is a universal resurrection, or an absolute No-saying that is an absolute Yes-saying, or an absolute Night that is absolute Day.

And this is the day of the resurrection of Anna Livia Plurabelle, repeating Dante's final voyage into the depths of the Godhead, as once again the scattered limbs or leaves of the universe become bound by love in one single "volume":

> So. Avelaval. My leaves have drifted from me. All. But one clings still. I'll bear it on me. To remind me of. Lff! So soft this morning ours. Yes. (628.6–9)

But as opposed to the final Yes of *Ulysses*, this Yes is followed by a summons to the divine Father and Creator:

> Carry me along, taddy, like you done though the toy fair! If I seen him bearing down on me now under widespread wings like he'd come from Arkangels, I sink I'd die down over his feet, humbly dumbly, only to washup. Yes, tid. There's where. First. (628.9–13)

Accordingly, this Leda, even as Yeats's, absorbs the power and the glory of the Godhead. But in this radical Catholic scripture or text, the "Infinite Goodness" finally passes into that *the* that Joyce believed is the weakest word in the English language:

> We pass through grass behush the bush to. Whish! A gull. Gulls. Far calls. Coming, far! End here. Us then. Finn, again! Take. Bussoftlhee, mememormee! Till thousendshee. Lps. The keys to. Given! A way a lone a last a loved a long the (628.12-17)

Now even if this conclusion is simultaneously the beginning of *Finnegans Wake*, its very sounding now reverses
that word that Joyce believed is the strongest word in the
English language, *God*. Joyce, who believed so deeply that
the inexplicable does not exist, did not choose this word
lightly, for it and it alone calls forth the absolute ground
that is the center of this apocalyptic crucifixion and resurrection. Yet now an apocalyptic resurrection is the resurrection of the Great Goddess, that Goddess who speaks
and acts in Anna Livia Plurabelle. But her apocalyptic
epiphany can occur only after and as a consequence of the
apocalyptic crucifixion of that Christ who is the Creator,
or that Christ who here bears the name of Here Comes
Everybody. Now the original sacrificial Jesus is wholly
embodied in the Body of the Goddess, and that Body is an
absolutely glorious Body, even while simultaneously being
the very body of the universe. So it is that the apocalyptic
crucifixion of the uniquely Christian God is here the apocalyptic resurrection of the uniquely Christian Goddess, just
as a uniquely Catholic mass is a historical and a cosmic
mass simultaneously, and hence a mass which is an epic
enactment of the cosmic history of Godhead and humanity. Not until *Finnegans Wake* does that mass undergo a
real and actual epiphany. If that epiphany is an apocalyptic
epiphany, it is an epiphany of the uniquely Catholic Christ,
or that Christ who is God and Goddess at once, and thereby
and only thereby humanity and deity at once.

CHAPTER SEVEN

The Protestant Jesus:
Milton and Blake

It has become historically clear that the Reformation was a consequence of the late medieval world, a world which when viewed as a whole has been called the Franciscan Middle Ages,[1] and surely Franciscan theology dominated that period, a theology which was not only an antispeculative or antimetaphysical nominalism, but also a theology which whether implicitly or explicitly was profoundly apocalyptic. This is clear above all in Peter John Olivi, who was the intellectual and charismatic center of the Franciscan Spirituals, and who believed that a new spiritualized Church would rule the world immediately prior to the final end of history. Luther himself deeply believed that the end of the world was immediately at hand, it is just because of this that Satan now dominates the world as never before, and Christ and Satan were equally real to Luther.[2] But the very apocalyptic advent of Satan releases a new and terrible *Anfectung*, a truly new *Angst* or despair, one shattering an established sacramental and penitential world. This new and overwhelmingly interior guilt, a primal ground of the Reformation, brought with it a truly new ultimacy of damnation and Hell. Already in his lectures on Paul's Epistle to the Romans, given in 1515–16, Luther made a fundamental theological breakthrough, and most clearly so in his understanding of the damnation of Christ:

> For even Christ suffered damnation and dereliction
> to a greater degree than all the saints. And his suf-
> ferings were not, as some imagine, easy for him. For
> he really and truly offered himself for us to eternal
> damnation to God the Father. And in his human
> nature, he behaved in no other way than as a man
> eternally damned to Hell. Because he loved God in
> this way, God at once raised him from death and
> Hell and thus devoured Hell. All his saints must
> imitate him in this ... [3]

Hence a uniquely Protestant imitation of Christ is the
renewal of the damnation of Christ, a renewal of the "curse
for us" of the Crucifixion (Galatians 3:13), just as this
crucifixion and this crucifixion alone is here the source of
justification or redemption. Yet if this is a crucifixion which
devoured Hell, it nevertheless released a totality of Satan
and Hell that had never been actual or manifest before,
and one that is perhaps the deepest ground of Protestantism. *Paradise Lost* is the primal epic of Protestantism, if
not of the modern world itself, and Milton is our purest
Protestant theologian, going far beyond Luther and Calvin
in his total negation of Catholic tradition. Milton's great
theological treatise, *De Doctrina Christiana*, is unique
insofar as it so fully conjoins a systematic and a biblical
theology, and even as he wrote it during the period when
he was composing *Paradise Lost*, it still remains our deepest commentary on that epic. Nothing is more theologically distinctive of both Milton the epic poet and Milton
the dogmatic theologian than his profound anti-
Trinitarianism. Anti-Trinitarianism was characteristic of
the Radical Reformation as a whole, but only realizes a full
theological expression in Milton. Such anti-Trinitarianism
is the inevitable consequence of a uniquely Protestant

faith in Christ, a Christ who is a purely kenotic or self-emptying Christ, and hence a Christ who cannot possibly share the essence of an absolutely sovereign and transcendent God.

Milton knew the absolute sovereignty and the absolute transcendence of God as it had never been known before, hence there can be no metaphysical knowledge of God whatsoever, for the absolute sovereignty of God is the absolute freedom of God, a freedom transcending all necessity. While Luther, too, broke with all metaphysical theology, he did not or could not break from ancient Christian Trinitarianism, even if, unlike Calvin, he had little taste for the Trinity. All too significantly, Milton understood the dogma of the Trinity as a deep assault upon the sovereignty of God, and hence upon God Himself, and at no point in the *Doctrina* is his biblical exegesis more compelling than in his demonstration of the absence of any real scriptural foundation for the dogma of the eternal generation of the Son of God, demonstrating on the contrary that such a generation could only be a temporal generation. For the Son was "begotten" by God, a generation taking place within the bounds of time, and one which has nothing to do with the essence of deity, for it was a consequence of the free decree of God.[4] God did impart something of His substance to the Son, but it could not have been His total essence, for the Father and the Son differ in essence, as is abundantly clear in the New Testament itself. Above all, the infinite essence or substance of God could not become incarnate, just as the supreme God could not empty Himself (Philippians 2:6): "But since he emptied himself of that form of God in which he had previously existed, if the form of God were taken to mean the essence of God, it would prove that he had emptied himself of the very essence of God, which is impossible."[5]

Indeed, for Milton, Christ is the beginning of the creation, and that could only mean that he was the first of the things which God created.[6] And that creation is an absolutely sovereign act of creation, for God produced all things not out of nothing but out of Himself.[7] *Creatio ex Deo* is an absolutely free and absolutely sovereign act, and in the *Doctrina*, although not in *Paradise Lost*, creation is the sole act of God the Father, that Father who is Godhead itself, and Godhead precisely as an absolutely free and sovereign Godhead. Nothing could be further from that Godhead than the crucified Christ, for even if Christ's nature is both divine and human, Christ totally died upon the cross, and not only both his soul and body died, but his divine nature succumbed to death as well as his human nature.[8] At no point was Milton more revolutionary theologically, a theological revolution inseparable from the epic revolution of *Paradise Lost*, as for the first time in both theological thinking and poetic language itself death is known not only as an ultimate but as a divine event, and an event that is the sole source of redemption. Certainly Luther was reborn in Milton; this was perhaps his only full theological rebirth, and if Milton is our only fully biblical theologian, that could only be because for Milton himself all human traditions, whether written or unwritten, are expressly forbidden.[9]

Nowhere in the world of theology can one find such a total commitment to *sola scriptura*. Even though Milton, like most theologians, could know scripture as a double scripture, the external scripture of the written word and the internal scripture of the Holy Spirit. For Milton the supreme authority is the authority of the Spirit, which is the internal and the individual possession of everyone.[10] All things are eventually to be referred to the Spirit and the unwritten word, but that is a word that is deeply present within each of us, and only that word alone can be our ultimate authority. Milton went far beyond Luther's doctrine of the priesthood of all believers, calling for the complete freedom of Christian liberty, for Christ's sacrifice abrogated the total Mosaic law, moral as well as sacerdotal and civil, and bestowed on Christians a total liberty freeing them from all human judgment as well as all civil or ecclesiastical coercion.[11] It is the external law which is abrogated by the crucifixion, a law that both Paul and Milton could know as a curse, but that abrogation is in fact a freeing of the true substance of the law, which is realized in that love of God and our neighbor as born in faith and in faith alone.

Now that we have learned to distinguish the Magisterial from the Radical Reformation, we can understand Milton as the supreme radical Protestant theologian. Here an individual and internal authority transcends all corporate and external authority, and spiritual authority can only be an individually enacted authority, open to all. If Milton's poetry is inseparable from the radically Protestant faith of Milton, then so, too, is Milton's poetry inseparable from Milton the radical political actor and thinker, and all too significantly Milton is our only major poet who was a major political actor. This occurred, of course, in the English Revolution, and if this was the revolution that inaugurated modern political revolution, it was the first political recognition of a common or universal humanity, just as it was the first fully political embodiment of an apocalyptic faith and energy. Only in the English Revolution is the Radical Reformation corporately embodied, and just as radical Protestant movements and sects were a driving power in that revolution, so, too, was was a truly new common language—a common language which could be an exalted language, as in the King James Version of the

Bible, and a common and exalted language that is the radically new epic language of *Paradise Lost*. While *Paradise Lost* is in deep continuity with the Western epic tradition, it nevertheless revolutionizes that tradition by calling forth a truly new epic totality. Now Dante's sacred universe is inverted, and inverted by way of a new ground in an ultimate and total fall. Milton's epic cosmos goes beyond even Dante's in calling forth a new and comprehensive order and harmony, but this order is now invisible, since it was lost with the fall, and now visible only to a blind prophet and seer who here knows himself as a reborn Moses, but a new Moses who can know creation only as exodus, for now the creation of the world can be known only as a response to the inevitable victory of Satan over humanity.

At no other point is there a deeper theological difference between *Paradise Lost* and the *Doctrina*. The epic poet can know a totality of the fall that is closed to the dogmatic theologian, just as he can know a totality of Satan that is alien to the theologian, and most alien to every theology that cannot know a divine death in the crucifixion. Milton knew the ultimacy of that death as did no previous theologian, a knowledge which is certainly a crucial ground of the radically new vision of Satan in *Paradise Lost*. For the first time in Christian vision, Satan is a truly glorious and majestic figure, the very center of a now totally fallen world. The fullest account of the creation in *Paradise Lost* occurs in Book VII, when Raphael at the request of Adam relates how and why the world was created, and we learn that this occurred in response to the victory of the Son of God and his legion of angels over Satan and the rebellious angels in a primordial war in heaven. Now "th'Omnipotent Eternal Father" declares that He will repair the detriment done by that rebellion, and do so by creating "Another World," out of which will arise a humanity that under long obedience will eventually rise to heaven:

> And Earth be chang'd to Heav'n, and Heav'n to Earth,
> One Kingdom, Joy and Union without end. (7:160)[12]

But as opposed to the *Doctrina*, now it is the Son of God who enacts the creation:

> And thou my Word, begotten Son, by thee
> This I perform, speak thou, and be it done:
> My overshadowing Spirit and might with thee
> I send along, ride forth, and bid the Deep
> Within appointed bounds be Heav'n and Earth,
> Boundless the Deep, because I am who fill
> Infinitude, nor vacuous the space.
> Though I uncircumscrib'd myself retire,
> And put not forth my goodness, which is free
> To act or not, Necessity and Chance
> Approach not mee, and what I will is Fate.
> (7:163–73)

Never was Milton either so audacious or so original as in this envisionment of the retirement of the Creator in the act of creation, a retirement necessitated by His fore-knowledge that Satan will defeat humanity, so that it is the Son who must actually effect the creation, even if the Son is thereby the agent of a now retired Creator. The Creator's own goodness could not be embodied in such a creation, and this by the free decree of an absolutely om-nipotent Creator, for the creation itself is a response to the primordial rebellion of Satan. Needless to say, nothing like this is present in the Christian tradition, and nowhere else is Milton's repudiation of that tradition more fully manifest.

But this repudiation arises from a truly new knowledge both of the Creator and of Christ, a Christ who is now and for the first time in Christian vision inseparable from Satan. Equally original and audacious is Milton's radically new vision of the rebellion of Satan, a rebellion occurring in response to a primordial enthronement of the Son, whereupon great Lucifer (the angelic name of Satan), and in imitation of the crowning of the Messiah, calls for a rebellion against the angels being eclipsed "under the name of King anointed":

> Will ye submit your necks, and choose to bend
> The supple knee? ye will not, if I trust
> To know ye right, or if ye know yourselves
> Natives and Sons of Heav'n possest before
> By none, and if not equal all, yet free,
> Equally free; for Orders and Degrees
> Jar not with liberty, but well consist.
> Who can in reason then or right assume
> Monarchy over such as live by right
> His equals, if in power and splendor less,
> In freedom equal? or can introduce
> Law and Edict on us, who without law
> Err not, much less for this to be our Lord,
> And look for adoration to th'abuse
> Of those Imperial Titles which assert
> Our being ordain'd to govern, not to serve?
> (5:787–802)

How close these words are to the political language of Cromwell's Latin Secretary when he was calling for a condemnation of monarchy by the whole world! Just as conservative England can know the English Revolution as the Great Rebellion, and a rebellion that is a demonic if not a Satanic rebellion, Milton could know the advent of

Satan as Satan as a rebellion against the newly established monarchy of the Messiah.

Certainly Milton's vision of the primordial enthrone- ment of the Son has only a very limited scriptural ground (Psalms 2 and 110 and Hebrews 1), but it is essential to Milton's radically new vision of Christ and Satan. For the first time in Christian vision, Christ and Satan can be known as a dialectical polarity, that deep and ultimate polarity which is the deepest ground of the dramatic and epic movement of *Paradise Lost*. Fully paralleling Lucifer's rebellion against a new Messiah is the Son's free accep- tance of incarnation and crucifixion as a necessary expia- tion of an inevitably forthcoming treason of humanity, a treason that embodies the rebellion of Satan and is nothing less than a cosmic victory of Satan. Now the Son is seen as being most glorious, in him all his Father shines sub- stantially, and in his face "Divine Compassion visibly appear'd," and an infinite love and grace (3:138–42).

> Behold mee then, mee for him, life for life
> I offer, on mee let thine anger fall;
> Account mee man: I for his sake will leave
> Thy bosom, and this glory next to thee
> Freely put off, and for him lastly die
> Well pleas'd, on me let Death wreak all his rage;
> (3:236–42)

This is the supreme filial obedience of the Son, offering himself as a sacrifice to fulfill the will of his Father, and to this obedience the Almighty can respond:

> Nor shalt thou by descending to assume
> Man's nature, less'n or degrade thine own.
> Because thou hast, though Thron'd in highest bliss

> Equal to God, and equally enjoying
> Godlike fruition, quitted all to save
> A World from utter loss, and hast been found
> By Merit more than birthright Son of God,
> Found worthiest to be so by being Good,
> Far more than Great or High; because in thee
> Love hath abounded more than Glory abounds,
> Therefore thy Humiliation shall exalt
> With thee thy Manhood also to this Throne;
> Here shalt thou sit incarnate, here shall Reign
> Both God and Man, Son both of God and Man,
> Anointed universal King; all Power
> I give thee, reign forever.
>
> (3:303–18)

Now even as the Son is the anointed King of Heaven, Satan is the Emperor of Hell, and just as the Son realizes his greatest glory by "merit" rather than by birthright, a merit impelling him to cross the vast chasm between earth and Heaven, and there to suffer and die alone for a wholly fallen humanity, so Satan, too, sits high on a throne of royal state in Hell, raised by "merit" to that evil eminence (2:5). Despair itself uplifts Satan high beyond hope, an exaltation realized by "merit" and an exaltation gloriously and dreadfully arising from his very descent and fall, so that Satan promises his demonic company that from their descent more glorious virtues and dread will arise than from no fall, and what they already have achieved they have achieved by "merit" (2:21). Then Satan resolves to venture alone across a terrible chasm between earth and Hell, and to expose himself alone to the ultimate terrors of Sin, Death, and Chaos, and finally to kenotically empty himself into a serpent so as to encounter and address that very humanity that is the object of the Son's absolute compassion. The truth is that the Son as Son, or as ultimate Messiah and Savior, is inseparable from the dark power of Satan. Only the triumph of Satan over humanity makes possible the atoning love and sacrifice of the Son, just as only the primordial enthronement of the Son makes possible the primordial rebellion of Satan. If that rebellion is the origin of Chaos, Death, and Sin, such a primordial fall is finally a *felix culpa* or fortunate fall, for just as only the voluntary death of the Messiah makes possible a reversal of the fall, only in that death is the Son truly glorious, only as a consequence of that death can the Son reign as God and Man forever.

We must never forget that *Paradise Lost* is a theodicy, written to assert "Eternal Providence" and to justify the ways of God to men (1:25). As is true of every genuine theodicy, this is finally a justification of evil itself, an evil employed as an instrument by the Creator to realize goodness and grace alone. Even Satan in Hell knows that God's providence seeks to bring forth good out of evil, so that Satanic labor must pervert that end (1:163–65). But the providence of God sanctions even that ultimately dark and terrible evil:

> but that the will
> And high permission of all-ruling Heaven
> Left him at large to his own dark designs,
> That with reiterated crimes he might
> Heap on himself damnation, while he sought
> Evil to others, and enrag'd might see
> How all his malice serv'd but to bring forth
> Infinite goodness, grace and mercy shown
> On man by him seduc'd, but on himself
> Treble confusion, wrath and vengeance poured.
> (1:211–20)

Human redemption and divine glory itself are inseparable from the eternal damnation of Satan, a damnation also embracing the great bulk of humanity. For even if no one is impelled by fate or destiny to sin, the freedom of obedience to God can be realized only by faith, and apart from that freedom everyone whatsoever is eternally damned. Yet actual redemption is possible only for the elect, just as actual liberty is possible only for those who are justified through faith and then adopted as the sons of God by having been made heirs by Christ.[13]

Paradise Lost is our supreme theodicy, going far beyond Augustine and Dante in its justification of evil, so that an Augustinian divine permission of evil (*The Enchiridion* 96) becomes a providential willing of fall and damnation. That fall is a fortunate fall and hence is inseparable not only from redemption but also from an ultimate and apocalyptic glory of God, a Glory of God which is finally realized only through the atoning and sacrificial death of Christ. But the actual name or title *Christ* never appears in either *Paradise Lost* or *Paradise Regained*. In the whole of his poetical works Milton employs it only in the title of *The Nativity Ode* and in the sonnet protesting against forcing consciences that "Christ set free," and this despite the fact that it occurs innumerable times in his prose, and above all so in *De Doctrina Christiana*. The truth is that Milton the poet could not pronounce the name of Christ, for a truly new Christ is enacted in Milton's epic poetry, a Christ who is a biblical and a uniquely modern Christ at once, and is so most clearly in his dialectical union with Satan. Here, it is Satan who most clearly embodies a uniquely Protestant conscience that is indistinguishable from *Anfectung* and *Angst*. Satan can transform the very love of God into an eternal damnation, as witness this soliloquy:

Hadst thou the same free Will and Power to stand?
Thou hadst: whom has thou then or what to accuse,
But Heav'n's free Love dealt equally to all?
Be then his love accurst, since love or hate,
To me alike, it deals eternal woe.
Nay curs'd be thou; since against his thy will
Chose freely what it now so justly rues.
Me miserable! which way shall I fly
Infinite wrath, and infinite despair?
Which way I fly is Hell; myself am Hell;
And in the lowest deep a lower deep
Still threat'ning to devour me opens wide,
To which the Hell I suffer seems a Heav'n.
                                                    (4:66–78)

A truly new epic self-consciousness is born in *Paradise Lost*, but now a wholly solitary and isolated self-consciousness, one that is most deeply embodied in Satan, and all of the soliloquies in *Paradise Lost* either occur in Hell or are inspired by Satan.

The Christian epic most deeply differs from Classical epic insofar as it is simultaneously an interior and a cosmic voyage. In *Paradise Lost* the two ultimate voyages are those of Satan and the Son of God. These are inseparable from each other, but it is Satan's voyage that effects an interiorization of humanity, a pure interiorization first occurring in Eve's temptation, one calling forth a purely negative consciousness, which alone can realize original sin. This negative interiorization is reversed by the passion and death of the Messiah, but that death is the damnation of Christ, and only that atoning and sacrificial damnation can reverse the eternal damnation of a universal humanity, just as only this death can realize an apocalyptic glory. But that glory is inseparable from an eternal damnation, for an eternal Hell is just as necessary to this apocalyptic glorification as is an eternal Heaven. If this apocalyptic Heaven is the eternal reign of that "Son both of God and Man," eternal Hell is not only an absolutely negative interiority, but one eternally deepening itself, even as an apocalyptic glory eternally exalts itself. Accordingly, Satan and the Son of God are truly dialectical opposites not only in the cosmic history of fall and redemption, but also in the apocalyptic goal and consequence of that cosmic history, an apocalypse in which absolute evil is just as necessary and essential as is absolute good, and in which an eternal Heaven is inseparable from an eternal Hell. Consequently, Satan is just as necessary as Christ to this apocalypse, for only an absolute evil makes possible the apocalyptic realization of an absolute good, and only the eternal power of that evil makes possible the eternal triumph of apocalypse itself.

Apocalyptic vision has always known the ultimate necessity of absolute evil or Satan. Just as there is no actual witness to Satan in the Bible until the advent of apocalypticism, no prophet before Jesus actually or fully speaks of Satan, just as no scripture in the world is so centered upon Satan as is the New Testament. Inevitably, a full renewal of the Bible, or of the Christian Bible, is a renewal of Satan. This occurs in the Reformation, and it continually recurs in the deepest expressions of Protestantism, but never so deeply as in the advent of full modernity. At no other point is Milton a deeper precursor of that modernity, as most clearly manifest in Milton's rebirth in William Blake, who not only could know himself as Milton reborn, but could know his own vision both as a radical transformation of Milton's vision and as its necessary and inevitable consummation and fulfillment. Certainly Blake is our most radical and original Christian visionary, and nowhere is he so radical as in envisioning God Himself as Satan. This radically original vision of Blake's was both a deep transformation of his own earlier vision and the consequence of a deep Christian conversion. Only then does Jesus become manifest as Christ in Blake's vision. Previously Blake could know Christ only as the repressed energy sealed in the tomb of the Christian church, whereas he had known Jesus as a pure innocence transcending all experience, except insofar as Jesus is that "I" who suffers in every woe and sorrow until our grief is destroyed ("On Another's Sorrow").

Perhaps no visionary has ever undergone so deep a transformation as Blake did while composing his manuscript epic *Vala* or *The Four Zoas* (probably 1795–1808), as can be seen in the very development and revisions of this epic wherein a primordial and "pagan" mythical language is transformed into a historical and Christian language. Thus the Crucifixion, which had been alien to the early Blake, now becomes the very center of a cosmic and apocalyptic history. Only now can Blake know the Crucifixion as the crucifixion of God, a death of God that is the death or "Self Annihilation" of Satan, and it is only by knowing that death that Blake can know the apocalyptic triumph of Christ. Earlier Blake had known the Christian or biblical God as Urizen, a tyrannical Creator whose law had enslaved a fallen humanity. Now the Creator is finally envisioned as a redemptive Creator, but redemption occurs only through the deepest and most total fall. Thereby Blake envisioned a radically new *coincidentia oppositorum*, a dialectical identity of Christ and Satan and Heaven and Hell, one that is actually realized historically and apocalyptically, and that is occurring here and now. The mythical figure who most deeply although most ambivalently embodies this movement is Luvah, the primordial energy or passion, whom the converted Blake can know as the sacrificial power of a universal crucifixion.

In the second night of *The Four Zoas*, which recounts Urizen's creation, Luvah cries out:

> "O Lamb
> Of God clothed in Luvah's garments! little knowest
>   thou
> Of death Eternal, that we all go to Eternal Death,
> To our Primeval Chaos in fortuitous concourse of
>   incoherent
> principles of Love & Hate."
>
> (99–104)

Here, Blake is struggling to create a new vision of the Crucifixion, a vision unveiling Calvary as a sacrifice of God to God, for the Lamb who is offered to the Creator is the final manifestation of the alienated and emptied God, as Blake appears to be saying in this late addition to the second night:

> For the Divine Lamb, Even Jesus who is the Divine
>   Vision,
> Permitted all, lest Man should fall into Eternal Death;
> For when Luvah sunk down, himself put on the robes
>   of blood
> Lest the State call'd Luvah shoud cease; & the Divine
>   Vision
> Walked in robes of blood till he who slept should
>   awake.
>
> (261–65)

No figure in the whole range of Blake's mythology has created more confusion and controversy than Luvah, a Luvah who is neither a consistent nor a clear figure in Blake's vision, and frequently embodies all the ambivalence of an initial burst of vision. Milton O. Percival, who believed that Luvah is the very substance of Blake's vision, has given us the best definition of this paradoxical figure:

> He is the point of man's departure from Eden, and the goal of his return. At the summit he is Christ; at the nadir he is Satan.[14]

Blake can name Luvah as Satan because Luvah has entered the "State of Death" (*Jerusalem* 49:67), for the Lamb of God can descend to redeem only when clothed in Luvah's robes of blood, and the daughters of humanity so greet the lamb in the late night eight of *The Four Zoas*:

> "We now behold ....
> Where death Eternal is put off Eternally.
> Assume the dark Satanic body in the Virgin's womb,
> O Lamb Divine! it cannot thee annoy. O pitying one,
> Thy pity is from the foundation of the World, & thy
>   Redemption
> Begun Already in Eternity. Come, then, O Lamb of
>   God,
> Come, Lord Jesus, come quickly."
>
> (239–45)

Yet it is in *Milton* itself that Blake gives us his clearest vision of the "Self Annihilation" of God. Only in this epic does Blake clearly portray himself as an enactor of apocalyptic revelation, as Milton enters his foot while Blake is walking in his garden, thereby not only passing on his prophetic mantle to Blake, but opening Blake to visionary depths that were closed to Milton himself, and are now called forth as a final apocalyptic revelation. In this epic, Milton is an embodiment of the redemptive Christ, as

Milton's vision of the Son of God's free acceptance of sacrifice and death is now envisioned as the deepest movement of a universal humanity, an "Eternal Great Humanity Divine" that is a cosmic and historical expression of a *coincidentia oppositorum*, a final and apocalyptic union of the warring polarities of a fallen Godhead. So, too, Milton's radical vision of the fall is now renewed, now known not only as the total fall of cosmos and history, but as an ultimate fall of Godhead itself, and it is precisely that fall that is reversed in the "Self Annihilation" of God. Accordingly, the Crucifixion is now and for the first time envisioned not only as a universal cosmic and historical process, but as the deepest movement in the Godhead, a movement that is primordial and apocalyptic at once, and therefore the self-sacrifice or "Self Annihilation" of God.

Now the heavenly assembly of *Paradise Lost* witnesses the original epiphany of the biblical God as the epiphany of Satan:

> He created Seven deadly Sins drawing out his infernal
>   scroll,
> Of moral laws and cruel punishments upon the clouds
>   of Jehovah
> To pervert the divine voice in its entrance to the earth
> With thunders of war and trumphets sound, with
>   armies of disease
> Punishments & deaths muster'd and number'd;
> Saying I am God alone
> There is no other! Let all obey my principles.
> (Milton 9:21–26)

This, of course, is in full continuity with the early Blake, but in *Milton* this epiphany of the wholly other and repressive God is finally inseparable from its very opposite, the epiphany of the "Self Annihilation" of God, as Jesus, the image of the "Invisible God," becomes its prey by being a curse, an offering, and an atonement (2:13), so that Jesus now in Milton goes to "Eternal Death," a damnation that is now revealed as an embodiment of Christ in Satan:

> I in my Selfhood am that Satan: I am that Evil One!
> He is my Spectre! in my obedience to lose him from
>   my Hells
> To claim the Hells, my Furnaces, I go to Eternal Death.
> And Milton said. I go to Eternal Death! Eternity
>   shudder'd.
>
> (14:30–33)

Now it is finally revealed that the self-annihilation of God in Christ is the self-annihilation of Satan, the sacrifice of the fallen and empty body of the Godhead, the very Godhead that is the repressive ruler of a wholly fallen world, and that is the final sacrifice, which is apocalypse itself. So it is that Milton or the atoning Christ in entering Satan can declare:

> Satan! my Spectre! I know my power thee to annihilate
> And be a greater in thy place, & be thy Tabernacle
> A covering for thee to do thy will, till one greater
>   comes
> And smites me as I smote thee & becomes my covering.
> Such are the Laws of thy false Heavns! but Laws of
>   Eternity
> Are not such: know thou: I come to Self Annihilation
> Such are the Laws of Eternity that each shall mutually
> Annihilate himself for others good, as I for thee.
>
> (38:29–36)

Milton, however, does not stand alone, for it is the initial expression of a dual and apocalyptic epic, whose larger and truly chaotic embodiment is *Jerusalem*, which is not only dedicated to "Jesus alone," but is finally the epic and apocalyptic movement of Jesus alone. In both epics, the "Human Imagination" is the "Divine Body of the Lord Jesus" (*Milton* 3:3; *Jerusalem* 5:59), an imagination realizing itself through the atoning and sacrificial movement of Luvah. This realization is reflected in the "Mundane Shall" of the cosmic heavens, which both records and embodies a total fall that is finally a kenotic or self-emptying reversal of itself.

Jerusalem opens with an epiphany of Jesus, whose spirit is the continual forgiveness of sin:

> I am not a God afar off, I am a brother and friend;
> Within your bosoms I reside, and you reside in me:
> Lo! we are One; forgiving all Evil; Not seeking
>   recompense!
> Ye are my members O ye sleepers . . .
>
> (4:18–21)

Now we are asleep in Ulro or Hell, but Jesus calls us to an awakening of "Eternal Death," which is nothing less than an awakening to "Eternal Life." Later, in the address to the Jews, we learn that all of us are united in one religion: "The Religion of Jesus: the most Ancient, the Eternal: & the Everlasting Gospel" (27). This is the religion that Satan has reversed:

> He withered up the Human Form,
> By laws of sacrifice for sin:
>   Till it became a Mortal Worm:
> But O! translucent all within.

>The Divine Vision still was seen
>Still was the Human Form, Divine
>   Weeping in weak & mortal clay
>O Jesus still the Form was thine.
>
>And thine the Human Face & thine
>The Human Hands & Feet & Breath
>   Entering thro' the Gates of Birth
>And passing thro' the Gates of Death
>
>And O thou Lamb of God, whom I
>Slew in my dark self-righteous pride:
>   Art thou returned to Albions Land!
>And Is Jerusalem thy Bride?
>   (27:53–68)

Consequently, the Divine family can declare:

>Mutual in one anothers love and wrath all renewing
>We live as One Man; for contracting our infinite senses
>We behold multitude; or expanding: we behold as one,
>As One Man all the Universal Family; and that One Man
>We call Jesus the Christ: and he in us, and we in him,
>Live in perfect harmony in Eden the land of life,
>Giving, receiving, and forgiving each others trespasses.
>He is the Good Shepherd, he is the Lord and master:
>He is the shepherd of Albion, he is all in all . . .
>   (38:16–24)

But we have become one with great Satan, enslaved to a cosmic but fallen "Selfhood," murdering the "Divine Humanity," until by "Self Annihilation" we come into Jerusalem. For the Lord Jehovah has bound the stars into a merciful order, bending the laws of cruelty to peace

(49:55). Here, too, Blake has transformed a fearsome Urizen into a merciful Jehovah, and Jehovah's salvation

> Is without Money & without Price, in the Continual Forgiveness of Sins
> In the Perpetual Mutual Sacrifice in Great Eternity! for behold!
> There is none that liveth and Sinneth not! And this is the Covenant of Jehovah:
> If you Forgive one-another, so shall Jehovah Forgive You:
> That He Himself may Dwell among you.
>
> (61:22–26)

Yet we are born a Spectre or a Satan, and must continually be changed into our direct contrary. If we do not have the religion of Jesus, we will have the religion of Satan, the "Wheel of Religion," and Jesus died because he strove against the current of this wheel (77:17). That is the death which is the center of this apocalyptic epic, and not only its center but its conclusion as well, a conclusion, which is an apocalyptic *coincidentia oppositorum*, a final and apocalyptic union of Christ and Satan.

But the apocalyptic body of Christ is the sacrificial and universal body of Jerusalem, a Jerusalem who undergoes a full and ecstatic union with the white and alien body of Jehovah in the illustrations on plates 96 and 99 of her epic, and the crucial text accompanying these illustrations records Jesus' final words to Albion or a universal humanity:

> Jesus said. Wouldest thou love one who never died
> For thee or ever die for one who had not died for thee
> And if God dieth not for Man & giveth not himself
> Eternally for Man Man could not exist for Man is love;

    As God is love: every kindness to another is a little
        Death
    In the Divine Image nor can Man exist but by
        Brotherhood.

                                            (96:23–28)

Thus the death of God is the self-sacrifice of God, a kenotic
emptying that is the embodiment of a total compassion,
the love that is finally the deepest depths of actuality itself. *Jesus* is the Christian name of those depths, just as
Jerusalem is the Christian name of their apocalyptic embodiment, an embodiment finally realizing a total union
with Satan. For *Satan* is the Christian name of an absolutely alien power—the deepest depth of a "Selfhood" that
is the alien and fallen Creator. Yet a total fall is finally a
fortunate fall. It alone makes possible an ultimate movement of love or sacrifice. That sacrifice is realized in God
alone, even if it is finally embodied in us all. Accordingly,
Jesus alone is God alone, for *Jesus* is the name of God's
apocalyptic death. That death is the death of Satan, yes,
but it is the sacrifice of an absolute compassion.

CHAPTER EIGHT

The Nihilistic Jesus:
Dostoyevsky and Nietzsche

Nothing is more characteristic of full modernity than the ravaging power of nihilism, one which is truly released in the French Revolution, although its seeds are far earlier, and Nietzsche, our greatest and purest nihilistic thinker, could know the origin of nihilism as occurring in the birth of Christianity itself. The late Nietzsche also could know the Christian God as the deification of nothingness, the will to nothingness pronounced holy. Even if Nietzsche finally came to know Christianity as a total reversal of Jesus, it was Jesus and Jesus alone who made possible such a reversal, and from this perspective it is Jesus who is the origin of our nihilism. Already Dostoevsky not only knew but deeply embodied this realization, and although Nietzsche only discovered Dostoevsky two years before his final breakdown, and never encountered his greatest work, he could write to George Brandes in 1888 that Dostoevsky's work is the most valuable psychological material known to him, even if it goes against his own deepest instincts.[1] But Dostoevsky is not only a great psychological writer, he is a luminously nihilistic one as well, and these dimensions of his writing are not only inseparably conjoined but a primal source of his overwhelming power. Dostoevsky, even as Nietzsche, is irresistible to us all. If only the twentieth century is a fully nihilistic age, Nietzsche and Dostoevsky are its purest prophets, and most clearly so in their nihilistic vision. Even though each of them gave his deepest power to opposing and reversing nihilism, it was precisely thereby that they called forth its deepest depths, which in their wake have overwhelmed humanity as a whole.

Nihilism was not fully born as a public movement until mid-nineteenth-century Russia. It was most influentially present in Turgenev's novel *Fathers and Children*, and here it is Bazarov's "Nihilism" that is the center of the novel, a source of a primal conflict between a radical new generation and its inherited world of values and ideas. This conflict became the dominant theme of the Russian novel of the 1860s,[2] and this was a world with which Dostoevsky deeply contended. Not only did it profoundly shape his own deepest writing, but it called forth his vocation as a Christian novelist. And surely Dostoevsky is not only our greatest but our purest Christian novelist, and perhaps our only genuinely Christian novelist as well. Nowhere in his writing are Christianity and nihilism more deeply intermingled than in that ultimately nihilistic novel that has been translated as *The Possessed*, *Devils*, and *Demons*. The Russian title *Besy* refers not to possessed but to possessors, here clearly possessors of an ultimately demonic power, and not demonic in a modern psychological sense, but rather demonic in the New Testament sense, as is clear in each of the novel's epigraphs. Theologically, "devils" is surely the more accurate translation, at least in the twentieth century, for these demonic powers are not simply evil traits or ideas, but rather a truly Satanic power, which Dostoevsky believed was virtually incarnate in the modern world. All too significantly this novel is a political and a theological novel at once, and it has been hailed as our greatest political novel, but here politics is a theological politics, as is true of the great nihilistic political movements of the twentieth century.

Christianity and nihilism are the ultimately contending powers in *Devils*, and while the opposition between them is ultimate, it is ultimate in a dialectical and not a dualistic sense, as in the New Testament itself. Yet, in *Devils*, genuine faith and pure or deep nihilism are never fully or even truly distinguished from each other. Each has a polar relation to the other, and not only a polar but a fully dialectical relationship, wherein the deepest expressions of nihilism are impossible apart from faith, just as the most genuine faith can be actually realized only in a fully nihilistic context or world. Above all, an imitation of Jesus here is inevitably a nihilistic imitation, and while this theme is foreshadowed in *The Idiot*, it is only in *Devils* that a renewal or rebirth of Jesus is a nihilistic rebirth. In the period when he was writing this novel (1869–1871), Dostoevsky was abroad, suffering intensely from both external adversity and internal assaults, for his epilepsy was at its worst, and while he was writing his epileptic fits increased in both their frequency and their intensity. Initially, moreover, he did not want to write this novel, but rather what he then and even later regarded as his greatest work, "Atheism," or "The Life of a Great Sinner," a project that was a primary core of all of his major novels.

Dostoevsky wrote in a letter in 1870 that his new novel would be his last, consisting of five large novellas completely independent of one another. While each novella would have its own title, the overall title of the novel would be *The Life of a Great Sinner*:

> The main question which will run through all the parts of the novel is the question that has tormented

me either consciously or unconsciously all my life—
the existence of God. In the course of his life, the
hero turns from atheism to faith, to fanaticism and
sectarianism, and then back to atheism.[3]

This hero becomes Stavrogin in *Devils*, and in early notes
to the novel, in which Dostoevsky speaks of Stavrogin as
everything, he provides a sketch of his character and situation:

Accumulation of wealth.
Emerging powerful passions.
Strengthening one's will power and inner strength.
Boundless pride, and his struggle against vanity.
The prose of life and a passionate faith which keeps
    overcoming it.
So that everybody will bow before me, while I shall
    forgive.
So as to fear nothing. Sacrifice one's life.
The effect of debauchery, a cold horror. A desire to
smear everybody with dirt.
The poetry of childhood.
Education and first ideals.
Secretly learned everything.
All alone, get ready for everything.[4]

What drives him most of all is what Nietzsche knows as
the Will to Power, and here, too that power is conceived
as the dethroning of God.
    A late note for the novel insists that the question as to
what ought to be considered "truth" is what this novel is
all about.[5] Certainly Stavrogin is its central hero, a hero
about whom all the other figures in the novel turn, for
Stavrogin is not only Dostoevsky's purest image of "The
Great Sinner," but also the deepest embodiment of that

"Atheism" that is the very incarnation of nihilism. Nevertheless, Stavrogin, even as Nietzsche's Zarathustra, is an embodiment of that unique will to power which is ultimately the act of sacrifice. The movement of sacrifice is the deepest plot of this and all of Dostoevsky's major novels. In *Devils* this movement is enacted by each of its major characters, except for that Pyotr Verkhovensky, who is its most literally nihilistic character. Indeed, it cannot be denied that *Devils* is in genuine continuity with a deeply Russian Orthodox tradition, in which the imitation of Christ is necessarily a kenotic act of sacrifice. As Joseph Frank notes, salvation for Dostoevsky always depends on the capacity of the prideful ego to surrender to the free self-sacrifice of love made on its behalf by Christ.[6] Frank also affirms that Dostoevsky is unique in European literature in centering his work upon the opposition between the "law of personality" and the "law of Christ," and that his genius consists precisely in his ability to unite these ultimately opposing laws.[7] Unquestionably, Dostoevsky's vision revolves about an ultimate *coincidentia oppositorum*, and if it comprehends a dialectical unity between Christianity and nihilism, it no less comprehends such a unity between the totally sacrificial Christ and the totally atheistic "Great Sinner."

No imaginative writer is so deeply given to the Incarnation as is Dostoevsky, an incarnation not only in the "flesh," but into the deepest depths of sin and damnation, so that the Incarnation for Dostoevsky is inevitably the Descent into Hell, a Hell incarnate in a uniquely human will to power. But the full and pure reversal of that power is the realization of salvation. Nowhere in our literature is salvation more profoundly ambivalent and paradoxical than it is in *Devils*, and while Stepan Trofimovich is the only one here who is literally given salvation, his is surely an ironic if not a comic salvation, and if this is the only happy death in the novel, it is also the most shallow one, and it pales into insignificance against the suicide of Stavrogin. Stavrogin truly is everything in this novel, and not only everything but everyone, for each of the major characters in the novel is a creation of Stavrogin's, just as each of them, again with the exception of Pyotr, enacts Stavrogin's destiny in his or her own distinctive way. Though this is a tragic destiny, the deepest question posed by the novel is whether or not such a tragic destiny is finally a redemptive one as well. Everything depends here upon our understanding of nihilism, for if this is a nihilism created by a uniquely modern atheism, it is thereby created by a uniquely modern will to power, embodied in all of the characters in the novel, and even, as he concedes, by the holy Tikhon. Yet it is Kirillov who most purely embodies such a will to power, and while, as Dostoevsky's notebook reveals Kirillov entered the novel only at a late stage of its composition, no other character of Dostoevsky's is so uniquely his own, just as no other character in our literature is so passionately and so purely in quest of redemption.

We are introduced to Kirillov as a notable civil engineer, a young man, as are all the "devils" in the novel, about twenty-seven years old, decently dressed, with dark hair and black, lusterless eyes. Immediately Kirillov declares that he despises conversation, as is confirmed in his odd, agrammatical speech, for the last four years he has seen very few people and spoken very little, later we learn that he is now impoverished, almost destitute, although he never notices his own poverty. Suicide is Kirillov's overwhelming obsession, one which has possessed him all his life, and when we first meet him, an untrustworthy character informs us that he rejects mo-

rality completely and supports the "latest principle" of
total destruction on behalf of the ultimate good, which
will demand the death of at least a hundred million.
Kirillov reluctantly accepts this depiction, but it assumes
a whole new meaning when he speaks for himself, for
then he reveals that he is an apocalyptic prophet, living
in expectation of the immediate coming of the total transformation of all and everything, when, as the Book of
Revelation declares, time will come to an end. Yet the
apocalypse can come only when one individual dares freely
to commit suicide. A truly free suicide has never yet
occurred, and while it is true that everyone most deeply
desires suicide, the fear of pain in the act of suicide and
its possible consequences in the next world have thus far
made a genuine suicide impossible. Indeed, true suicide
is possible only by way of an absolute freedom. Such
freedom is the goal of all humanity, and its realization in
true suicide will effect a physical transformation of both
humanity and the world.

Eastern Christianity differs most decisively from Western
Christianity in its ultimate goal of a universal deification.
God became man that we might become God. That final
goal is apocalypse itself, and thus Kirillov can confess:

> Life is pain, life is fear, and man is unhappy. Now
> all is pain and fear. Now man lives life because he
> loves pain and fear. That's how they've made it.
> Life now is given in exchange for pain and fear, and
> that is the whole deceit. Man now is not yet the
> right man. There will be a new man, happy and
> proud. He for whom it makes no difference whether
> he lives or does not live, he will be the new man.
> He who overcomes pain and fear will himself be
> God. And this God will not be.[8]

Later Kirillov realizes that everything even now is good, so he prays to everything, and when he is challenged by Stavrogin, that one human being he reveres, he reveals the depths of the uniquely Russian Christianity that he so deeply possesses:

> "I am good."
> "With that I agree, incidentally," Stavrogin muttered
>   frowningly.
> "He who teaches that all are good, will end the world."
> "He who taught it was crucified."
> "He will come, and his name is the man-god."
> "The God-man?"
> "The man-god—that's the whole difference." (p. 238)

The ancient Eastern Christian goal of Godmanhood was resurrected in Russia in the late nineteenth century, above all by the young Vladimir Soloviev, who had a deep impact upon Dostoevsky. Soloviev sought for a truly new God-manhood that is the consequence of the advent of a new Christianity, a Christianity that it was Russia's destiny to reveal to the world. Dostoevsky himself was a prophet of such a Christianity, and in this novel the prophetic voice of a radically new Christianity is most clearly embodied in the voice of Kirillov, despite his "atheism." For Kirillov's is a paradoxical atheism, one in which Kirillov knows that God doesn't exist and can't exist, and yet God is necessary and must exist (p. 614). Only Kirillov now truly knows this, unless it is also known by Stavrogin, and thus it is Kirillov's destiny to be the savior of the world:

> I'll begin and end, and open the door. And save. Only this one thing will save all men and in the

next generation transform them physically; for in the present physical aspect, so far as I have thought, it is in no way possible for man to be without the former God. For three years I have been searching for the attribute of my divinity, and I have found it: the attribute of my divinity is—Self-will! That is all, by which I can show in the main point my insubordination and my new fearsome freedom. For it is very fearsome. I kill myself to show my insubordination and my new fearsome freedom. (p. 619)

Shortly thereafter Kirillov does kill himself, and whether or not this was actually a free suicide, we can never know. But that Kirillov is a deep embodiment of Dostoevsky himself we cannot doubt, and just as each so deeply believed that he was tormented by God throughout his life, each was given epileptic fits inducing an ecstasy in which time almost comes to an end:

There are seconds, they come only five or six at a time, and you suddenly feel the presence of eternal harmony, fully achieved. It is nothing earthly; not that its heavenly, but man cannot endure it in his earthly state. One must change physically or die. The feeling is clear and indisputable. As if you suddenly sense the whole of nature suddenly say: yes, this is true. . . . You don't forgive anything, because there is no longer anything to forgive. You don't really love—what is here is higher than love! What's most frightening is that it's so terribly clear, and there's such joy. If it were longer than five seconds—the soul couldn't endure it and would vanish. In those five seconds I live my life through, and for them I would give my whole life, because it's worth it. (p. 590)

Perhaps Kirillov's atheism is most paradoxical in his faith in Christ. Like Prince Myshkin in *The Idiot* in his response to Holbein's portrait of the dead Christ, he knows Christ as that one supreme being who was crushed by the laws of the universe:

> Listen to a big idea: There was one day on earth, and in the middle of the earth stood three crosses. One on a cross believed so much that he said to another: "This day you will be with me in paradise." The day ended, they both died, went, and did not find either paradise or resurrection. What had been said would not prove true. Listen: this man was the highest on all the earth, he constituted what it was to live for. Without this man the whole planet with everything on it is—madness only. There has not been one like *Him* before or since, not ever, even to the point of miracle. This is the miracle, that there has not been and never will be such a one. (p. 618)

Kirillov's deepest goal is to imitate Christ, an imitation that will be not simply a renewal of Christ, but a reenactment of the once and for all salvation of all humanity in the crucifixion of Jesus. That crucifixion is the realization of apocalypse itself, but it has been reversed by the terror of death, and can be renewed only by an absolute act of "Self-will." If such Self-will can occur only in an absolute freedom, it can be realized only in an absolute act of self-negation or self-emptying, a self-negation that is Self-negation, and therefore a suicide that is deicide itself, or a suicide in which Self-will is Self-negation. Kirillov knows that God comes to an end in the moment of an absolutely free suicide, or in the moment of crucifixion. But that is the moment in which time comes to an end, that one moment which is apocalypse itself. Therefore that moment's renewal is the renewal of the redemption of Christ, and therefore the renewal of the "suicide" of Christ, who died wholly by his own will. And that will is the self-negation, or the self-emptying, of "Self-will" itself.

Kirillov is just thereby the holiest figure in *Devils*, even more humanly holy than Tikhon himself. He is also its most sacrificial figure, and the only one who freely and actually gives himself to others. Yet Kirillov is actually a creation of Stavrogin's, an enactment of only one dimension of Stavrogin's life. Even as Kirillov's suicide is finally inseparable from Stavrogin's wholly destructive suicide, his self-will is equally inseparable from Stavrogin's self-will, the deepest self-will Dostoevsky created. Indeed, faith and self-will are far more deeply conjoined in Stavrogin than in Kirillov, and so much so that each is indistinguishable from the other. So that Kirillov himself can remark of Stavrogin that if he believes, he doesn't believe that he believes, and if he doesn't believe, he doesn't believe he doesn't believe. And if Stavrogin himself embodies an absolute freedom, that freedom is indistinguishable from an absolute slavery. No one else in this novel is so profoundly driven, and perhaps this is why he has such an overwhelming impact upon all others, an impact wherein Stavrogin truly does become all in all. Yet Stavrogin's heroic power is inseparable from his abject degradation and humiliation, one in which he invariably humiliates himself. If thereby Stavrogin is a "holy fool" in a deeply Russian sense, again and again playing that role with others, it is just his maddest actions that have the greatest effect upon this world.

We must concede that Stavrogin is not a fully realized character in *Devils*, but this is true in greater or lesser degree of all of Dostoevsky's major characters. None of his novels is a truly finished novel, for Dostoevsky is our only major artist who never fully completed a major work of art. No doubt his vision defies such resolution, and while Dostoevsky is like all other great artists in transcending all full or real theological identification, he was theologically tormented as have been few other artists, and most so in his creation of his greatest characters. Dostoevsky, moreover, is our most dramatic novelist, embodying a dramatic power that rivals that of Sophocles and Shakespeare, and this a drama driven by the sheer power of its actors or characters, a power wholly transcending every possible interior power or decision. While it is tempting to think that Dostoevsky is a tragic novelist, this is not fully true. His novels never have genuinely tragic resolutions, not only because of the deep ambiguity of all of Dostoevsky's endings, but also because these endings are never truly resolutions at all, except insofar as they effect a radical disruption of every movement that occurs in these dramas. Such a disruption most clearly occurs in the conclusion of *Devils*, an ending which is the suicide of Stavrogin, and the concluding sentence informs us that the medical men, after the autopsy, completely and emphatically ruled out insanity.

Shatov, the all-too-reluctant atheist who believes that Russia is messianically destined to regenerate the world in the name of a new God, confesses that he was originally inspired by Stavrogin, who as a teacher had raised him from the dead. Then he learned that Roman Catholicism had transformed Christ into Antichrist and had destroyed the whole Western world. Certainly, at that time, Stavrogin was a deep Christian believer, who had declared that if mathematicians could demonstrate that Christ lay outside of truth, he himself would still prefer to remain with Christ rather than with truth (p. 249). Even very late in the novel,

Pyotr Verkhovensky, the leader and inspiration of that tiny nihilistic cell that presumes to be the nucleus of a world-wide communistic and nihilistic revolution, confesses that Stavrogin is not only the leader but the sun, the sun who is that Ivan Tsarevich who will be the emperor of a new nihilistic world (p. 421). Yet this is an emperor who in his very ennobling power has been broken throughout his life. In the long-suppressed chapter "At Tikhon's," Stavrogin confesses that he has been subject to hallucinations, hallucinations in which he actually sees the devil, and unlike Ivan Karamazov he fully affirms that he believes in a personal devil, even if he does not and cannot believe in God. In response to this, the holy Tikhon maintains that absolute atheism stands on the next to last rung of the ladder of perfect faith, thereby inducing Stavrogin to draw forth a written confession recording the foulest deeds of his life.

Now we are taken into his life of debauchery in Petersburg, and Stavrogin confesses his full responsibility for the suicide of a young girl whom he had befriended, a suicide following what must have been Stavrogin's rape of this holy innocent, a rape impelling her to cry that she had killed God. Throughout all this, Stavrogin records an incredible pleasure that he realized through his most despicable acts, but a pleasure inseparable from a guilt that drives him to one of his most self-destructive acts, his marriage to the crippled and retarded Marya Lebyadkina, a marriage that he finally reveals to all, thereby creating an explosion that finally ends this demonic drama. But, in this perspective, is it not true that Stavrogin's life, the life of a great sinner, is an inversion and reversal of the life of Christ? Nevertheless, and even thereby, it is a repetition of the life of Jesus, an imitation of Jesus in a degraded and inverted kenotic sacrifice, one now calling forth and exalting rather than banishing and defeating devils, thereby embodying a pure nihilism that is an inversion of the compassion of Jesus, and yet, impossible apart from just such an inversion and reversal. Inevitably, Stavrogin deeply believes in Satan, and belives in Satan if only because of his faith in Christ, a Satan who is finally defeated in the crucifixion of Jesus, but who is nonetheless resurrected when that crucifixion is inverted and reversed, a resurrection embodying the virtually infinite power of the Will to Power, which itself is a full reversal of the compassion of Christ. Yet this will to power is finally crushed in Stavrogin's suicide, and in the death or destruction of all these devils here, save Pyotr or a purely demonic St. Peter, a destruction going far beyond the path of solitude and mortification recommended by Tikhon to Stavrogin, and going beyond it as an ultimate and final act, and an act that is a reversed and inverted repetition of the ultimate act of redemption that the Christian knows to have been realized in the destruction and death of Christ.

Nietzsche can claim to himself, in his notebook, that he is the first perfect nihilist of Europe, who has even now lived through the whole of nihilism, to its very end, finally leaving it behind, outside himself.[9] Nevertheless, his is the time of the advent of nihilism, a nihilism that is the ultimate logical conclusion of our values and ideals, for every purely moral value system ends in nihilism; and even as this has already occurred in Buddhism, a "second Buddhism" is now overwhelming the West. But Nietzsche knows Christianity as the origin of our nihilism. At bottom Christianity has always been a yearning for "Nothing," just as the Christian God is the deification of nothingness. When one places life's center of gravity not in life but in the "beyond"—in nothingness—one deprives life of its center of gravity altogether.[10] Yet Nietzsche came very deeply to believe that Jesus himself denied everything that today is called Christian:

> If one were to look for signs that an ironical divinity has its finger in the great play of the world, one would find no small support in the *tremendous question mark* called Christianity. Mankind lies on its knees before the opposite of that which was the origin, the meaning, the right of the evangel; in the concept of "church" it has pronounced holy precisely what the "bringer of the glad tidings," felt to be *beneath* and *behind* himself—one would look in vain for a greater example of *world-historical irony*.[11]

The truth is that Nietzsche revered Jesus as he did no other historical figure, perhaps because he all too gradually came to know him as the very opposite of Christianity. This occurred most decisively in his final years or months of creativity, in a period that marked his breakthrough to a radical new hope and expectation, and one which is inseparable from the full advent of nihilism itself. Nietzsche could sign himself as "Dionysus" or "The Crucified" when he was falling into madness, and he could know the Crucified Christ as even today the most subline of all symbols,[12] but that is a crucifixion that has been reversed by Christianity, and reversed by knowing the crucifixion as the portal to an eternal and heavenly life. In *The Antichrist*, Nietzsche purports to tell us the genuine history of Christianity, unveiling the very word *Christianity* as a profound misunderstanding, for there was only one Christian, and he died on the cross. Moreover, Jesus' gospel or "evangel" died on the cross: "What has been called 'evangel' from that moment was actually the opposite of that which *he* had lived: *"ill* tidings," a *dysangel"* (§ 612). Whereas Christianity has immersed its followers in an inevitable and total guilt, the most terrible and devastating guilt ever known in history, the language of guilt is totally absent from the language of Jesus. The "glad tidings" of Jesus is precisely the announcement that "sin"—any distance separating God and man—is abolished (§ 606). And the consequence of the gospel of Jesus is not "faith," but a radically new *praxis,* an evangelical practice of total compassion for all. The life and death of Jesus is nothing other than this practice, only this practice leads to God: "indeed, it *is* 'God' " (§ 607).

Hence the God of Jesus is the very opposite of the God of Christianity, and so much so that it is not "God" at all, or nothing that could be known as God in Christianity. Yet Christianity's total reversal of Jesus is an ultimately nihilistic act, reversing the fullness of his life into a heavenly nothingness, and reversing the ecstatic joy of his gospel into an ultimate guilt and *ressentiment.* So it is that Nietzsche finally came to know Christianity as the one great curse, the one great innermost corruption, the one great instinct of revenge, and the one immoral blemish of humanity (§ 656). But Nietzsche also knows his own time as the last day of Christianity. If our time is the time of the full advent of nihilism, this very nihilism is the end of our greatest error and catastrophe, for the catastrophe of Christianity finally unveils itself as a pure nihilism, and Nietzsche can know that very revelation as the high point of humanity. Now even if Nietzsche knows Jesus himself as the very opposite of a Christian nihilism, and the one true opposite of a pure nihilism in all our history, the true and original Jesus can only be known by the Christian as a nihilist, a total transformation of Jesus already beginning in the New Testament itself, and above all so by Paul. For it is Christian faith which transforms the life and death of Jesus into *dysangel, a dysangel which is* nihilism incarnate, and precisely thereby an obedience to and communion with the uniquely Christian God that is the will to nothingness pronounced holy. The Christian

God is an absolute No-saying, and the only pure and total No-saying in our history; nevertheless this absolute No-saying finally makes possible an absolute Yes-saying, and does so when the Christian God is dead.

Already Jesus could know that death, and could know it by proclaiming and living the end of sin and guilt. But the modern realization of the death of God is the true advent of nihilism, a nihilism that is the consummation of Christianity, and consequently the consummation of the Christian God. In this perspective, who could doubt that Nietzsche's madman, who proclaims the death of God, is intended to be a rebirth and renewal of Jesus?

> "Whither is God" he cried. I shall tell you. *We have killed him*—you and I. All of us are his murderers. But how have we done this? How were we able to drink up the sea? Who gave us the sponge to wipe away the entire horizon? What did we do when we unchained this earth from its sun? Whither is it moving now? Away from all suns? Are we not plunging continually? Backward, sideward, forward, in all directions? Is there any up or down left? Are we not straying as through an infinite nothing?[13]

If there has never been a greater deed, and if all who are born after this deed will be part of a higher history than all history hitherto, and precisely because of this deed, is that deed not that ultimate act that is first embodied in Jesus, and embodied equally in his life and death? Nietzsche thereby could know Jesus as the greatest and truest revolutionary in history. If the death of God is the great dividing line in world history, that is the death which is embodied in Jesus, whose death called forth the greatest counterrevolution in history, the birth of Christianity itself.

Nietzsche unveils the Christian Christ and the Christian Jesus as truly nihilistic, as the embodiment of the purest and most total nihilism in history. That nihilism is not only created by Christianity but occasioned by Jesus, and perhaps even necessitated by Jesus, and inevitably so for Jesus

> stands outside all religion, all cult concepts, all history, all natural science, all experience of the world, all knowledge, all politics, all psychology, all books, all art,—"his knowledge" is *pure foolishness* precisely concerning the fact that such things exist. *Culture* is not known to him even by hearsay, he does not need to fight it—he does not negate it. The same applies to the state, to the whole civic order and society, to work, to war—he never had any reason to negate "the world"; the ecclesiastical concept of "world" never occurred to him. To negate is the very thing that is impossible for him.[14]

Who else but Jesus is wholly incapable of any negation? And if this is the Jesus whom Nietzsche came to know, is it possible to imagine a greater revolutionary, even if this is a revolution that can brook no negation whatsoever? Yet this Jesus immediately calls forth a negation of himself, and a negation of himself in a Christian nihilism, a nihilism that is an absolute flight from Jesus, and therefore a flight to the uniquely Christian God.

Now this God is dead, a death of God which is the death of the uniquely Christian God, and this is that one event which for Nietzsche is an absolutely redemptive event, even if it inevitably calls forth the fullness of nihilism, a nihilism that is the very tomb of God. Such a nihilism is impossible apart from the Christian God, and can truly or fully be manifest only as a consequence of the death of God. Nietzsche was obsessed by God—obsessed as no other thinker in history, and his obsession was centered upon the death of God. That death releases a total nihilism, that is the nihilism which is the nihilism of a uniquely nihilistic God, whose greatest impact comes with the death of God. Nietzsche is our greatest nihilistic thinker precisely because he so deeply knows the uniquely Christian God. His knowledge is not only inseparable from but identical with a realization of the death of God, a realization which is finally the realization of an ultimate and total redemption, and thus a realization which finally transcends nihilism itself. Certainly this was Nietzsche's hope, and even a claim which he privately made for himself, and if Nietzsche's deepest energy and power were given to a reversal of nihilism, such a reversal could only be a total reversal of Christianity, but a reversal which even thereby calls forth, and inevitably, calls forth the original Jesus.

Few theologians, and perhaps even fewer New Testament scholars, have read *The Antichrist*. But how could they dare to read it, a work that goes so far beyond even our most radical biblical scholarship and criticism? *The Antichrist* was the last work Nietzsche gave to the world, and just as it was intended to be the first part of his ultimate work, *Revaluation of All Values*, we can understand it as the work that most decisively and most finally broke Nietzsche himself, and even if Nietzsche scorned martyrs, he is the one true martyr of pure thinking itself. Can we look upon his descent into madness as a Kirillovian suicide, a free suicide that is a consequence of an "absolute freedom," and precisely thereby an ultimately redemptive act? Nietzsche, in spite of himself, revered Jesus and looked upon the symbol of the Crucified Christ as the most sublime of all symbols. Is his descent into Hell a repetition of

the crucifixion, a renewal of the crucifixion in a totally
nihilistic age and world? Certainly we cannot doubt that
Nietzsche could so profoundly understand nihilism just
because of his realization of the death of God, and just as
this could be said of Dostoevsky as well, both Dostoevsky
and Nietzsche understood Western Christianity as a pure
nihilism, and a nihilism finally exploding with the end of
that Christianity itself. But is that ending the beginning of
a truly new Christianity, as Dostoevsky so deeply believed?
A beginning that itself would be a rebirth and renewal of
the original Jesus? Only in the context of that rebirth could
the Christian or the Western Christian Christ be known as
a purely nihilistic Christ, a dead and empty Christ who is
the embodiment of an ultimate nothingness, an all-too-
actual nothingness that is the actuality of an ultimate guilt
and revenge, but a revenge and guilt that die with the
renewal of Jesus, or with the absolute reversal of the Christian or the Western Christian God.

Or should we look upon Nietzsche's final breakdown as
an enactment of a Stavrogian self-destruction, a perfectly
sane and even free suicide that is the self-emptying or self-
abrogation of an all-too-human will to power, a will to
power that now unveils itself as just what it is? If Nietzsche
ever gave us a pure portrait of the total absence of the will
to power, this surely occurs in his depiction of Jesus in
The Antichrist, and if this is a Jesus who is totally incapable of negation, it is the death of this Jesus that calls
forth the pure nihilism of Christianity, a nihilism which is
pure negation and negation alone. Both Nietzsche and
Dostoevsky profoundly understood that nihilism can be
truly negated only at the very center of its own deepest
ground, and such negation can occur only when nihilism
has fully and finally realized itself. This realization occurs
as a consequence of the death of God, and even as that

death finally ends everything that Europe and the West have known as God, it precisely thereby promises an ultimate liberation. How odd that Dostoevsky and Nietzsche, our purest nihilistic thinkers and visionaries, could each have been inspired by such an ultimate hope, a hope impossible apart from this very nihilistic vision. And if each again and again enacted an ultimate death, and an ultimate death which is a nihilistic death, can that death be dissociated from the original death of Jesus? Nietzsche could understand that death as giving birth to a pure and total nihilism, the most devastatingly destructive nihilism in history, but one which is revealed as such only in the death of the uniquely Christian God. That death not only reveals our nihilism, but enacts it, and enacts it as a finally redemptive event, an event releasing the totality of the will to power, yes, but finally the will to power is the Will to Power, a will that is an absolute No and an absolute Yes at once.

CHAPTER NINE

The Buddhist Jesus

Only one figure in world history is truly comparable to Jesus, and that is Siddhattha Gotama, whose name embodies as great a historical revolution as has ever occurred, and even as Gotama's own *dhamma* or way was revolutionary in its own historical world, it has certainly become so throughout Asia as a whole, just as it promises to be so in our new universal world. While it is true that it is extraordinarily difficult if not impossible for the historian to recover the original way of Gotama, and that scriptures recording that way did not come into existence until perhaps five hundred years after Gotama's death, Buddhism has never known those ultimate controversies that have been generated by theological and historical quests for the original way of Jesus, just as Buddhism is innocent of those lethal and pathological conflicts that have ever accompanied the deepest and most powerful historical expressions of Christianity. But just as modern historians have fully demonstrated the comprehensive historical transformations of Christianity, modern scholars have called forth seemingly comparable historical transformations of Buddhism. Yet Buddhists can know radically diverse ways of Buddhism as being quite simply the way of the Buddha, just as they can know even the purest and most exalted philosophical expressions of Buddhism as being quite literally the *dhamma* or *dharma* of Gotama or Gautama. Mahayana and Vajrayana Buddhism are commonly known to the Western scholar as being at a virtually infinite distance from early Buddhism, but Buddhist scholars and thinkers, at least in non-Theravada circles, can know them as pure expressions of the original *dharma*.

From a Western and Christian perspective, nothing is more revolutionary in Buddhism than its primal doctrine of *anatta* or selflessness. *Anatta* is at the very center of Gotama's way, it is likewise at the center of every subsequent expression of Buddhism, and so much so that at no other point may one more fully discover the unity of Buddhism. Whereas non-Buddhist interpreters of Buddhism tend to understand this doctrine in isolation from other doctrines of Buddhism, it would appear that Buddhists themselves understand this doctrine not simply in conjunction with other Buddhist doctrines, but rather as a realization of the totality of *dhamma* or *dharma*, and so much so that *anatta* can be understood as *dhamma* itself. Could this be a way for the Christian into the totality of the Kingdom of God? Often we are instructed that *paticca-samuppada*, or the chain of causation or dependent origination, is the primal doctrine of Buddhism. But this is clearly a way of realizing that there can be no center or origin of any kind, and cannot be not simply because everything is dependent upon everything else, but more deeply because everything whatsoever is profoundly conditioned by antecedent factors, and therefore nothing whatsoever, and above all not our own center or "I," has any independent or integral existence whatsoever. Only the absolutely unconditioned or nirvana is free of the chain of causation or dependent origination. Even if nirvana is *sunyata* or absolute emptiness, it is empty because it is empty of causation or origination, and such emptiness is absolute freedom or enlightenment.

Buddhists who are open to Christianity have little diffi-
culty in identifying Jesus as a Buddha or enlightened one,
but few Christians have identified Buddha as a Christ or
Messiah, and then only all too tenuously and fragmentarily,
most commonly seeing Gotama as a precursor of Jesus, or
Buddha as an Eastern image of Christ. Yet if the Buddha is
not simply the title of the Enlightened or the Liberated,
but is the actual way to an absolute liberation, a liberation
that is finally the liberation of all, then the Christian must
inevitably know the Buddha as the Christ, and perhaps
thereby finally know Gotama as Jesus. Only in the deepest
expressions of Western mysticism and Western apocalypticism has the West known a real and actual totality.
But the very horizon of the Buddha inevitably calls forth
totality itself, even if an absolutely empty totality, a totality negating every possible interior center or ground, and
even every exterior ground that is not totality itself. Indeed, there is nothing in Christianity truly comparable to
Buddhist *dharma*. Nowhere in Christianity is there a way
that is an ultimate self-emptying that is quite simply and
only reality itself, or a selflessness calling forth the emptiness of all and everything, or a totally conditioned or
samsara that at bottom is nirvana itself. Nevertheless, each
of these resolutions deeply resonates with a truly apocalyptic way, for is not the ending of all given totality the
advent of a new and final totality, and an apocalyptic way
of ending or death the resurrection of that death itself, and
the triumph of the Kingdom of God over death and darkness a realization of that God in Christ who will be all
in all?

Each of these apocalyptic motifs is far more clearly
present in Buddhism than in Christianity, or in the manifest historical expressions of Christianity. So it would not
be amiss to pose the question if it is possible that the

Buddhist Sangha knows Jesus more deeply than does the Christian Church, and perhaps truly knows the original Jesus by knowing the original Gotama. Only Buddhism and Christianity know their founders as the very way which they teach, a way that is an absolute compassion and finally the depths of reality itself. But Christianity knows that reality as the depths of the Godhead, a Godhead wholly absent in Buddhism, and far more deeply absent in Buddhism than in any other religious way or tradition. Perhaps nothing is so distinctive about Buddhism than is this absence, and an absence that is not simply an absence or an eclipse of God, but far rather an absence precluding the very possibility of the presence of God, and precluding it in its own deepest power and depths. Yet Buddhism is surely not atheistic, and not atheistic because here there is no negation of God, nor even the possibility of the negation of God, for ultimately in Buddhism there is no negation whatsoever. While Buddhism does intend to dissolve every source of pain and suffering, a pain and suffering *(dukha)* which are quite simply conditioned existence, the thirst *(tanha)* that Buddhism dissolves is a bondage or will to conditioned existence, and it is present nowhere but in the deepest depths of our own illusion. Even an openness to a beyond is a distraction from that illusion. All such openness must perish if liberation is to occur, so no opening can here occur to what the Western and the Christian world has known as God.

One of the most decisive differences between Buddhism and Christianity occurs in their purely theoretical or conceptual expressions. No founder has ever so purely condemned a purely theoretical thinking as did Gotama. And no other way has evolved a pure thinking that is so wholly conjoined with pure meditation. At no other point is there a deeper difference between Christianity and Buddhism. While something truly comparable to a Buddhist meditational thinking is surely present in Paul and the Fourth Gospel, this is lost with the advent of philosophical theology in the early patristic fathers, and lost if only because it is so deeply grounded in late Classical or Hellenistic philosophy, a philosophy that is wholly removed from the world of the Bible, and that Paul could know as the very antithesis of faith. So it is that Christian philosophy arose as a truly polar or dichotomous thinking, one in profound tension between its poles in Athens and Jerusalem. Even if Augustine and Aquinas could seemingly harmonize those poles, they are truly and finally dichotomized with the advent of nominalism and the modern world. No such opposition or polarization is found anywhere in genuine Buddhist thinking, a thinking which, unlike Christianity, evolved its own purely cognitive or conceptual ground. Buddhism created a pure and comprehensive logic that is at once a purely Buddhist logic and the most advanced and systematic logic ever known in the world until the advent of a purely mathematical logic in the nineteenth century.

While the Christian might be baffled or offended at the absence of God in Buddhist thinking, an absence fully realized in the deepest and purest expressions of Buddhist thinking, such an absence of even a trace of pure transcendence is surely inseparable from the very purity of Buddhist thinking, which is wholly closed to the very possibility of apprehending an essential and intrinsic "other," and therefore closed to the possibility of being open to the essential and final transcendence of God. For Buddhism can know an absolute presence, an absolute presence that is the Buddha, and even if absolute presence is absolute absence or absolute emptiness, that is an emptiness that is all in all, thereby precluding any possibility of either the presence or the realization of "God." Although it is true that modern Buddhist thinkers have been drawn to the mystical thinking of Meister Eckhart, discovering in an Eckhartian Godhead the absolute nothingness of sunyata itself, in this perspective not only is Godhead beyond God, but God is the self-negation of Godhead or the "absolute One."[1] It is not insignificant that such Buddhist thinkers have been deeply drawn to the theological language of kenosis or a divine self-emptying, a self-emptying which is the self-emptying of absolute nothingness itself, an absolute nothingness that is absolute presence and absolute absence at once. But in the horizon of that nothingness the Christian God can be manifest or known only as the self-negation of an original totality of nothingness.

At no point are modern Buddhism and modern Christianity more deeply estranged from each other than in a Buddhist apprehension of an original totality that is all in all, thereby not only necessitating a Buddhist "atheism," but also making possible a Buddhist apprehension of the transcendence of God as a self-negation of an original totality of absolute nothingness. But this is an apprehension calling forth a uniquely Buddhist understanding of the kenotic Christ, a Christ whose incarnation and crucifixion is the self-negation of the original self-negation of God, and therefore a kenotic and even historical realization of the self-negation of absolute nothingness. Such an understanding of the kenotic Christ also makes possible a kenotic understanding of the apocalyptic Jesus, for then the eschatological proclamation and parabolic enactment of the Kingdom of God could be understood as the realization of the self-negation of the Kingdom of God, or a realization of the self-negation of Godhead itself. Then the self-negation of an original self-negation of absolute nothingness could be understood as the realization of absolute nothingness. Such a realization is not a primordial realization as in Buddhism, a realization dissolving every possibility of Godhead itself, but rather a realization of the absolute reversal of the Godhead, a reversal which is the apocalyptic ending of the Godhead, yes, but precisely thereby a consummation rather than a dissolution of the Godhead.

Whereas Buddhism forecloses the possibility of either the apprehension or the realization of "otherness," an otherness inseparable from the primordial transcendence of the Christian God, that foreclosure is itself inseparable from the primordial totality of nirvana or sunyata. If Buddhism is our purest and most comprehensive realization of that totality, the Buddhist dhamma or dharma is the most total embodiment of that totality. In this perspective, Christian apocalypticism is the pure opposite of Buddhism, and is so if only because it embodies an apocalyptic and even absolute ending, an ending which is the real and actual opposite of a primordial and absolute "nothingness," and is so if only because of the sheer actuality of its occurrence. Nowhere is that occurrence more manifest than in what the Christian knows as the ultimacy of the crucifixion, and even if this is an absolute ending which is an absolute beginning, it nevertheless is absolute ending, an ending which is the "death of God." But the crucifixion is the consummation of Jesus' eschatological proclamation and parabolic enactment of the Kingdom of God. If the crucifixion fully parallels the absolute "selflessness" of the Buddha, it nevertheless is an absolute act or enactment, and therefore the true opposite of an absolute and primordial nothingness. Therefore an apocalyptic Kingdom of God can be known as the true opposite of a Buddhist nirvana or sunyata, just as the kenotic Christ can be known as the true opposite of the kenotic Buddha, and even Jesus known as the opposite of Gotama.

Yet even as an apocalyptic Christianity can know a *coincidentia oppositorum* between crucifixion and resurrection, or an ultimate death and an ultimate life, the possibility is therein established for us of knowing a *coincidentia oppositorum* between the Buddha and Christ or between Gotama and Jesus. Such a *coincidentia*, of course, could only be a dialectical identity of real opposites, but if Jesus and Gotama are real opposites, they are open to such a dialectical unification. Certainly the ways they embodied are open to such an identification, ways which are not only ultimate kenotic or self-emptying ways, but ways which center upon a compassion that is all in all, yet a compassion that is wholly unreal apart from either an apocalyptic enactment or an interior and kenotic dissolution. That Jesus enacted such an apocalyptic ending we cannot doubt, or cannot doubt apart from a Gnostic ground. But whereas a kenotic dissolution became normative in Buddhism, an apocalyptic enactment became peripheral and heretical in Christianity, and above all to all established and orthodox forms of Christianity. Accordingly, it is orthodox Christianity that is most distant from Buddhism, and this is true of both Catholic and Protestant orthodoxies, whereas the most radical expressions of Christianity, as witness Eckhart and Blake, are seemingly fully open to Buddhism. Of course, a radical and apocalyptic Christianity is not simply identical with Buddhism, such an identity could only be a dialectical identity, and therefore an identity inseparable from a profound and ultimate opposition.

Such an opposition is surely present in Jesus' proclamation of the full and actual advent of the Kingdom of God, an advent that could be nothing less than total presence, and the total presence of totality itself, a totality that he alone could name and enact as the Kingdom of God. In the perspective of Gotama's way, such a total presence could only be a total absence, a total absence realized in the enactment of *anatta*. Such an enactment could only be a disenactment, a disenactment not simply of the possibility of Godhead itself, but a disenactment which is a dissolution of every center, and thus the dissolution of the possibility of a real and actual presence. Perhaps only in a Buddhist perspective can we realize the totality of the total presence Jesus enacted, a totality that is the true opposite of a Buddhist totality of total absence. If that absence is *anatta* or *paticca-samuppada*, that absence truly is an absolute nothingness from the perspective of the totality of the Kingdom of God. And if Godhead is more truly absent from the Buddhist way than from any other way, that is precisely the horizon in which we can apprehend the possibility of a total presence, a total presence that is the true opposite of total absence. Nevertheless, and precisely by the way of that pure opposition, the possibility is called forth of knowing the total presence of the Kingdom of God, a total presence that has never been known by Christian dogmatics itself, if only because Christian dogma has been inseparable from the absolute transcendence of God, a transcendence that forecloses the possibility of total presence.

Christian dogma has always been estranged from the apocalyptic acts and language of Jesus, and even if that estrangement has been profoundly challenged by the deeper expressions of Christian mysticism and Christian apocalypticism, this has only deepened the mystery of the eschatological or the apocalyptic Jesus, as witness the wholly elusive identity of Jesus in either an Eckhart or a Blake. Yet in knowing Jesus as the true opposite of Gotama, and in knowing the Kingdom of God he enacted and proclaimed as the true opposite of a Buddhist nirvana, it is possible thereby to unveil both Jesus and the Kingdom of God, and to do so by way of realizing a dialectical relationship between nirvana and the Kingdom of God and between Gotama and Jesus. Both an apocalyptic Kingdom and a Buddhist nirvana are totality itself, a totality whose realization is the derealization of everything else, a derealization that is an absolute ending, an ending of everything that is "other" than nirvana or the Kingdom of God. So likewise both Christianity and Mahayana Buddhism know their founders as being themselves the totality of everything which they enacted or called forth, so that just as the Christian Jesus is the Christ even as the Buddhist Gotama is the Buddha, Christ is finally the totality of the Kingdom even as the Buddha is finally the totality of nirvana. Orthodox Christian Trinitarianism refuses Christ as the totality of the Godhead, just as orthodox Buddhist Trinitarianism refuses the *Nirmana-kaya*, or the "assumed body," of the Buddha, as the totality of Buddhahood. Yet an orthodox Christian Trinitarianism is truly distant from the New Testament, just as an orthodox Buddhist Trinitarianism is truly distant from ancient Buddhist scriptures. In each, Trinitarianism has been a primal instrument whereby both Buddhism and Christianity have distanced themselves from their origins.

Perhaps the deepest heresy of Meister Eckhart was his refusal to admit real distinctions within the Godhead, a refusal which is comprehensively reenacted in Hegel's purely dialectical philosophy. Hegel's trinitarian thinking is the rebirth of an ancient heretical dynamic monarchianism or Sabellianism in which the Father or the Creator is ultimately the Son or Christ. Thus Hegel and Eckhart refuse every final distinction between the eternal generation in the Godhead and the kenotic incarnation of Godhead or Spirit. Christian orthodoxy could condemn both Eckhart and Hegel as atheists because they refuse the absolute immutability of God, and do so precisely in knowing the ultimate self-emptying of God, a self-emptying that quite simply is the Incarnation. The Christian dogma of the Trinity only gradually evolved as a way of mediating between monarchianism and an Arianism denying the full deity of the Son of God. Just as it shared with a Neoplatonic monarchianism an apprehension of the impassivity and the immutability of the Godhead, it shared with Arianism a real distinction between the Father and the Son. Hence it could know a kenotic movement of passion and death only as occurring in the humanity and not in the divinity of Christ. Augustine, in his treatise on the Trinity, can go as far or further than any orthodox theologian in declaring that the Lord of glory was crucified: "because it is quite correct to talk even of God being crucified—owing to the weakness of the flesh, not to the strength of godhead" (1:28).[2] This is as close as Christian orthodoxy has come to affirming that God is crucified. But clearly here God is crucified only in the flesh or the humanity of Jesus, while remaining absolutely impassive and immutable in Himself.

Only Christianity among the world religions has been fully and finally dogmatic, and certainly Buddhism is not dogmatic in the Christian sense. But just as the original Jesus is eclipsed in orthodox Christianity, Gotama is largely eclipsed in Mahayana Buddhism; yet Mahayana Buddhism calls forth, as orthodox Christianity does not, the original way of its founder. Certainly *anatta* or selflessness is fully embodied in all forms of Buddhism, a selflessness which in Mahayana Buddhism is an identification with the Buddha, an identification which is all in all. Thereby the Buddha can be known and realized as totality itself. Even if a Buddhist totality is an absolutely empty totality, it can thereby be known as a reversal of the totality of the

Kingdom of God, but precisely therein in full continuity with the Kingdom of God. In Buddhist scriptures there is a full integration between the language of Gotama and the purely aniconic imagery of nirvana and sunyata, whereas in the synoptic gospels there is a deep and ultimate discord between the ecstatic joy of Jesus' eschatolological proclamation and enactment and the sheer horror of his passion and crucifixion. That horror scarcely is relieved by the all-too-fragmentary and contradictory New Testament accounts of the resurrection, and the passion story, not the resurrection, is the deep center of the synoptic gospels. Nothing like this is truly present in Buddhism. Its closest analogue is Gotama's refusal to immediately pass into nirvana upon realizing enlightenment, a refusal issuing from his decision to mediate the way of enlightenment to others, and Gotama's death, when it finally comes, is a moment of absolute peace and calm. At no other point is there a deeper contradiction between Christ and the Buddha or Jesus and Gotama, and if death is finally unreal in Buddhism, the death of the Crucifixion is absolute and ultimately real in Christianity, and a death that is inseparable from the triumph of the Kingdom of God.

Now if nirvana or sunyata is an absolute presence that is an absolute absence, the triumph of the Kingdom of God is realized only through the brutal horror of an ultimate suffering and death. Jesus is our only prophet, apart from Second Isaiah, who employed a language of total joy, but that joy culminates in a total horror—a horror foreseen by the fourth servant song of Second Isaiah, which is surely why the Book of Isaiah was the primary scripture for those primitive Christian communities out of which the synoptic gospels evolved. If nirvana can truly and purely be known as absolute nothingness, then the full and final actualization of the Kingdom of God can be known as occurring in the crucifixion itself, and a crucifixion which is the crucifixion of the Lord of glory, a crucifixion not only of the body or flesh of Jesus, but a crucifixion of God, and a crucifixion realizing the final or apocalyptic Godhead of God. The New Testament itself reverses this crucifixion in its images of resurrection, but neither the New Testament nor any subsequent Christian visionary can enact an actual story of the resurrection. The only real action or plot the Christian can narrate is the passion story, for the passion and the death of God are the deepest center of Christianity.

Yet that death and passion are the final realization of the Kingdom of God, a Kingdom of God that only here is fully and finally embodied, for even if that death calls forth the full advent of Spirit, Spirit is the resurrected Christ, a resurrection which is the universalization of the crucifixion. Buddhism can know a full reversal of that resurrection, a reversal in which passion and death fully and wholly disappear. But even the most exalted Christian art has never been able to envision the actuality of the resurrection, an actuality that is overwhelming in Christian images of the crucifixion. Yet Buddhist art has fully envisioned the absolute calm of the Buddha, the calm of an absolute nothingness or sunyata. That Buddha that is absolute nothingness can be known as a full and pure reversal of the crucified Christ, a pure and full reversal that has been impossible in Christian art and thinking, so that Buddhism can know the resurrected Christ as Christianity cannot, and even know Gotama as a pure reversal of Jesus. Christian Gnosticism is deeply enlightening at this point, for if it reverses the crucified Jesus into the purely spiritual and docetic Jesus, and does so by knowing crucifixion as resurrection and only resurrection, it thereby releases a profound loathing for cosmos and time that is wholly alien

to Buddhism, just as it realizes an absolute dualism that is
the very antithesis of Buddhism, a Buddhism which has
wholly and finally transcended dualism as has no other
tradition in the world. Certainly the Buddha is not a dualistic "other" of body and flesh as the Gnostic Christ
surely is. The Gnostic or purely spiritual Christ can never
be named or envisioned as compassion itself, but the Buddha is inevitably known as absolute compassion, and an
absolute compassion that is all in all.

Accordingly, there is a deep and pure correlation between Christ and the Buddha, just as there is between
Jesus and Gotama, and even if this is a correlation of pure
opposites, it is precisely thereby that Christ and the Buddha are dialectically united. The Kingdom of God that Jesus
enacted and proclaimed has become an ultimate and im-
penetrable mystery in the Christian and the Western world.
This is the very world that ever increasingly has come to
know an ultimate and absolute nothingness, a nothingness
which surely parallels a Buddhist nothingness, even if it is
wholly alien to compassion and calm, and embodies a
finally alien chaos that is truly absent from every Buddhist
horizon. Thus it is that Nietzsche, our greatest nihilistic
thinker, was profoundly drawn to Buddhism in his final
years, and perhaps in his early period as well when he was
so deeply affected by Schopenhauer. While Nietzsche could
know both Buddhism and Christianity as pure expressions
of nihilism, he judged Christianity to be an ultimate curse,
whereas Buddhism embodies and actual serenity and hap-
piness. Yet this is the Nietzsche who knew Jesus as the
very opposite of Christianity, and thereby he could know
Jesus as being in full continuity with Gotama, and above
all so in his full freedom from *ressentiment*. But the total
absence of *ressentiment* is the total presence of compassion, a pure absence of *ressentiment* that in Buddhism is

anatta, and an *anatta* that is finally nirvana or sunyata. Christianity has known an absolute compassion only insofar as it has known the crucifixion, and in knowing the crucifixion it has known the absolute compassion of God, but that compassion is actually and finally realized only in this ultimate death.

Thus the crucified Jesus, and only the crucified Jesus, is the full and actual opposite of Gotama the Buddha. If the way of Gotama is the way of nirvana, the way of Jesus is the way of the cross, and even the way of the cross in its ecstatic celebration of the full and final advent of the Kingdom of God, an advent finally realized in crucifixion, and realized in that crucifixion that is the "death of God." Consequently, if Buddhism embodies a dissolution of every possible presence of God, a dissolution embodied originally in Gotama himself, that is a dissolution which is actually enacted in the crucifixion, and enacted by that God who *is* Jesus, but who is fully and finally Jesus only in the crucifixion, a crucifixion actually and finally enacting an absolute compassion. Nevertheless, that dissolution can be understood and envisioned as a full analogue to the Buddha's enactment of *anatta*, an enactment which is a disenactment of a conditioned existence, and above all a disenactment of any and every possible center of conditioned existence. But is not the crucifixion the dissolution or disenactment of the center of Jesus' existence, and not simply the center of his human weakness as Christian orthodoxy affirms,[3] but rather the disenactment of his deepest center, a center that he himself could know and proclaim as the Kingdom of God?

Virtually all synoptic scholars have judged that the most authentic of the final sayings of Jesus is his anguished cry on the cross—"My God, my God, why have you forsaken me?"—a cry that Christian orthodoxy can understand as being intended to represent the death of our soul,[4] but one that Christian devotion and Christian meditation have enacted as the death of God, a death of God in Christ in this ultimate and absolute act that is the one source of redemption. Yet, so likewise, the Buddha's enactment of *anatta* is the one source of final liberation in Buddhism, and even if a Buddhist liberation is an absolute peace and a Christian liberation is the way of the cross, each is an absolute negation of an old Adam or an old humanity that is an absolutely conditioned existence. Both Augustinianism and Buddhism understand an absolutely conditioned existence as the real and intrinsic opposite of liberation, even as both in their radically different ways can know that the deepest source of our bondage lies wholly within. Buddhism knows our deepest within as a pure emptiness or nothingness, Augustinianism knows the deepest center of a wholly fallen humanity as the pure deficiency or the pure nothingness of sin. And if it is Jesus who first unveils the total emptiness of sin, and does so by his very enactment of the Kingdom of God, it is Gotama who first unveils the emptiness of all conditioned existence, and does so by his very realization of nirvana.

We can apprehend Gotama's death or pari-nirvana as being fully and wholly at one with the way which he taught, so that the total peace of his death is in full continuity with the total liberation which he enacted. From this perspective there is a profound chasm between Jesus' proclamation and enactment of the total triumph of the Kingdom of God and the awesome and horrible death that was his own destiny, and at no other point is there a greater gulf between Jesus and Gotama. Nothing in Buddhism is truly comparable to Christianity's ultimate centering upon the crucifixion, unless it is a Buddhist realization of *anatta* or sunyata as an absolute nothingness. But an absolute nothingness is an absolute totality, a totality that all given or manifest expressions of Christianity have refused as occurring in the crucifixion itself. If only at this crucial point, modern Buddhist thinkers and perhaps the Buddhist tradition itself have been far more open to the deep center of Christianity than has the Christian tradition and virtually the whole body of Christian theology, thereby knowing an ultimate and final self-negation as occurring in the Buddha, a self-negation that is the realization of nirvana or sunyata. But that self-negation is the negation of the deepest depths of illusion, an illusion arising from every possible apprehension of an actual and integral center, a center that is not simply the ground of *asmita* or ego-consciousness, but the ground of what Christianity knows as the absolute transcendence or the absolute "I AM" of God. That Buddhism cannot know such an "I AM" is not simply because Buddhism dissolves every possible interior "I," but also because it dissolves every possible center, and does so most deeply in its own purest embodiments.

Yet radical Christianity can know the crucifixion as the self-emptying or the self-annihilation of God, and ironically did so most fully at the very time when a truly historical Jesus was first being discovered. Hegelian thinking embodies the kenotic Christ more fully and more universally than any other thinking, just as a Blakean vision more openly and more finally embodies a kenotic Jesus than any other vision, but each is grounded in the absolute self-negation of the crucifixion, a crucifixion that is all in all. Indeed, at no other point are Christian thinking and Buddhist thinking more fully in harmony with each other than in a realization of an absolute self-negation. But whereas Buddhist thinking has known such self-negation from its very beginning, Christian thinking has known it only in a radically apophanic mysticism or in a truly atheistic consciousness and world. These are the Christian worlds that are most open to Buddhism, and just as a radically apophanic Christian mysticism has been a radically Neoplatonic or Eastern mysticism, as in Dionysius, Erigena, and Eckhart, a Christian "atheistic" thinking and vision has been most profoundly directed against that Christian God who is an absolutely sovereign transcendence, or that God who establishes the greatest possible distance between Buddhism and Christianity.

Nothing is more alien to orthodox Christian thinking than the kenotic or self-emptying movement of the Godhead. Augustine accepted the reality of that movement, but he could not accept it theologically as an actual movement of an absolutely immutable Godhead, but only as the servanthood of the humanity of Christ, just as Barth's modern dogmatics could know election or predestination as God's making His own Son to be sin for us, wherein Christ is the only one fully rejected or damned, but that rejection is wholly inseparable from the absolute triumph of Christ.[5] Of course, both Augustine and Barth were closed to the apocalyptic Jesus, a closure fully manifest in all orthodox expressions of Christian theology. Yet it is a closure precisely thereby to the synoptic language of the Kingdom of God, and if that is the language that most decisively distinguishes Jesus from all ancient prophets, it is also a language that is deeply alien to all orthodox Christian theology. And perhaps because that theology is most deeply grounded in the absolute sovereignty and the absolute transcendence of God, a transcendence foreclosing the possibility of an actual dawning or an actual apocalyptic realization of the Godhead, and therefore foreclosing the possibility of an actual dawning of the Kingdom of God. Here, the transcendence of God is the true "other" of any possible nirvana, but also and precisely thereby the true "other" of apocalypse itself, and most clearly the "other" of a crucifixion that is not finally resurrection and resurrection alone.

Only if the crucifixion can be understood as the full and final realization of Jesus' eschatological proclamation and enactment can we apprehend a Jesus who is apocalyptic and kenotic at once. But thereby we can apprehend a Jesus who is in full continuity with Gotama, and even know the Buddhist Gotama as a way of return to the original Jesus. Just as Gotama's calling forth of *anatta* is the very path to an ultimate liberation, Jesus' enactment of the dawning of the Kingdom of God is an enactment of ultimate liberation. This liberation is inseparable from the dawning of the deepest depths of God, depths whose actualization not only challenges but disenacts all previous epiphanies of God, and so much so that his primal words and acts are inseparable from a deep and ultimate offense. Of course, all genuine prophets have ever induced a deep offense, and if the Christian knows Jesus as the greatest and most ultimate of the prophets, that cannot be dissociated from the most ultimate offense, an offense above all to everything that faith, apart from Jesus, can know as God. Thereby we can know a genuine continuity between Jesus and Gotama. Not only did Gotama negate the deepest traditions of his own world, and negated them in their deepest ground, but his own way is inseparable from that negation, and most deeply so in its realization of ultimate liberation. Even if Jesus was crucified solely at the behest of Roman imperial authority, his crucifixion was an ultimate offense to Jewish tradition, and to Jewish revelatory and legal tradition, as Paul knew so deeply, and all too significantly the cross or the crucifixion is the most profoundly offensive symbol in the history of religions.

Nothing in Buddhism is capable of such an offense. In the Far East Buddhism has been offensive to Confucian tradition. But Buddhism and Confucianism eventually entered into a genuine synthesis. The deepest symbolic, meditational, and theoretical expressions of Buddhism realized a genuine embodiment in neo-Confucian philosophy and praxis, and Far Eastern Buddhism is now virtually inconceivable apart from a Confucian ground. Nevertheless, Buddhism is offensive to Christianity, and above all offensive to Christian faith in God. This offense is not unrelated to the ultimate offense embodied in Jesus, an offense induced by a transformation of the radical transcendence of God into the radical immanence of God, a transformation that is an inevitable consequence of a full and final apocalyptic enactment. Now even if both transcendence and immanence are alien categories in Buddhism, from a Christian perspective, and perhaps from a Christian perspective alone, Buddhism must appear as a transformation of transcendence into immanence, or a transformation of the Godhead into nirvana or sunyata. Thereby the Buddha even can be known to the traditional Christian as the Antichrist, and the Buddhist way as the way to an ultimate nothingness and death. And even as Freud could name the death instinct as the "nirvana principle," Buddhism has inevitably been known in the West as a pure nihilism, and nihilistic above all in its quest for nirvana. Thus, if Christianity and the West must know Buddhism as "atheistic," such an atheism is a pure and total immanence, an immanence inseparable from a pure and total negation of God.

But is not such negation present in the original Jesus, who in enacting the full advent of the Kingdom of God therein and thereby enacted the final fulfillment of the revelation of God, a fulfillment that could only be the ending of every previous revelation of God? Accordingly, here is a genuine *coincidentia oppositorum* between Jesus and Gotama, the one enacting the ending of revelation and the other enacting the impossibility of revelation itself, the one enacting a total transformation of a total transcendence into a total immanence, and the other enacting a total transformation of an absolutely conditioned samsara into an absolutely liberated *anatta* or nirvana. And just as an absolutely empty *anatta* is sunyata or nirvana, an absolutely empty transcendence is the final triumph of the Kingdom of God, a Kingdom of God that is all in all, even as an absolute nothingness is all in all. Yet the Kingdom of God is all in all only in that absolute event that is the crucifixion, even as sunyata is all in all only in an absolute emptying of consciousness, an emptying that is the dissolution or the derealization of all conditioned existence, just as an apocalyptic Godhead or omega is the consummation of the dissolution or derealization of primordial or transcendent Godhead itself. Thus the "kingdom" of God is the fullness of Godhead itself. But that fullness is only the consequence of an absolute act of emptying, a kenotic emptying of divine transcendence itself, and one that actually occurs in the crucifixion of the Lord of glory.

Just as crucifixion is wholly alien to Buddhism, so Godhead itself is alien to Buddhism, even absolutely alien to Buddhism, so that if Gotama is more innocent of deity than any other paradigmatic figure in our history, he therein truly is the opposite of Jesus, but an opposite who is a *coincidentia oppositorum* with the crucified Jesus. A Gotama who is wholly innocent of God is in full coincidence with that Jesus who embodies and enacts the death of God. Even if they are opposites of each other, and are so most deeply in their relation to Godhead itself, each enacted a dissolution or derealization of a transcendence that is the very "other" of an absolute and total presence, and equally so if that total presence is a total absence. Accordingly, the total absence of *anatta* is in full correlation with the total presence of the Kingdom of God. If *Anatta* is an ultimate dissolution or derealization, so likewise is a Kingdom of God that is an emptying of transcendent ground in the total presence of Godhead itself, a presence that Jesus proclaimed and enacted as the dawning of the Kingdom of God, but a dawning that is consummated only in the crucifixion. Consequently, the crucifixion is the death of God, the death of the God of glory, but precisely thereby a final consummation of the Godhead.

While the Buddhist Gotama is the true opposite of the Christian Jesus, he is precisely thereby the Buddhist Jesus, and above all the Buddhist Jesus in his very realization of *anatta*. Even if that realization is derealization, it is a derealization or dissolution realizing totality itself. While that totality is an absolute nothingness, it is totality precisely because of that. If such a totality is present only in Buddhism, its initiation was embodied only in Gotama. Yet an actual embodiment of an absolute transformation of transcendent Godhead was initiated only by Jesus. Jesus alone is the initial embodiment of the self-annihilation or the self-emptying of God, just as Jesus alone is the enactor of the full and final advent of the Kingdom of God. What could possibly be the relationship between Kingdom of God and nirvana, or between sunyata and Kingdom of God? Can each in its actual realization be an absolute nothingness or an absolute emptiness? Or an absolute emptying of transcendence itself? True, a Buddhist emptiness is a primordial emptiness, whereas an apocalyptic "emptiness" is the final and total presence of Godhead itself, a Godhead that is totally absent from absolute nothingness. Yet is it possible that in a Buddhist perspective we can know the uniquely Christian God as the self-negation of an absolute nothingness, as the self-negation of sunyata or nirvana? Is that why the Christian can know an absolute compassion only by way of an actual realization of crucifixion, only by an actual participation in the crucifixion of the Lord of glory? If transcendent Godhead itself is the self-negation of absolute nothingness, is that self-negation itself the embodiment of an absolute sacrifice or compassion, but one that is consummated only in an apocalyptic crucifixion? For if Gotama is Jesus, or Jesus is Gotama, then the Kingdom of God is the reversal of absolute nothingness, just as the self-negation of absolute nothingness is an absolute act of sacrifice and compassion.[6]

The Anonymous Jesus

If Jesus comes to us as one unknown, without a name, then not only is his an anonymous humanity, but he can be heard only by an anonymous humanity, an anonymous humanity that perhaps only now is being fully embodied in our midst. The Buddha, too, is purely and totally anonymous, and necessarily so insofar as the Buddha is the pure and total embodiment of *anatta*, an *anatta* that is nameless just because it is selfless, but here a namelessness that is all in all. So likewise Jesus' anonymity is all in all, and just as Christianity can know the name of Jesus as the deepest name of everyone, so that Here Comes Everybody is the apocalyptic return of Jesus, all the names of history are Jesus' names, but actually are so only in an apocalyptic totality. Thus, if Buddha is the name of no one, Jesus is the name of everyone, but only an everyone who is a new Adam or a new humanity, and new precisely by way of the crucifixion. This is that ultimately final event releasing a truly new humanity, but a humanity that is wholly anonymous from the perspective of an old humanity, just as *anatta* is truly nothing from the perspective of samsara. Yet what is the real difference between an anonymity that is no one and an anonymity that is everyone, or between a primordial nothingness and an apocalyptic nothingness? Is the name of Jesus itself a decisive clue to this difference, one that is inseparable from an apocalyptic enactment, and

therefore inseparable from the final enactment of the Kingdom of God?

Is Christianity itself finally inseparable from a primal
ground in an anonymous Jesus? Both the Pauline and the
Johannine traditions could know the human Jesus as a
virtual anonymity, even as Christian orthodoxy knows the
humanity of Jesus as a fully abstract humanity, and radical
Christianity knows Jesus as a universal self-emptying energy and power. Hegel himself deeply believed that as a
consequence of the crucifixion the original Jesus has wholly
and finally disappeared, and is resurrected only in an absolutely new and universal self-consciousness that is the final
realization of Absolute Spirit. *Absolute Spirit* is the
Hegelian name of the Kingdom of God, a Kingdom of God
that is the actual consequence of an ultimate and final
kenosis or self-emptying, or a kenosis that is the apocalyptic transformation of absolute transcendence into absolute
immanence. Nietzsche's proclamation of the death of God
is deeply Hegelian at this crucial point, and for Nietzsche
it is Gotama and Jesus who inaugurated the reversal of
resentiment, a *resentiment* that he could know as the very
origin of our interior "I."

If an anonymous Jesus is what Blake hailed as "The
Eternal Great Humanity Divine," it is an anonymous Jesus
who is the axis of our history, or the absolute dividing line
between an old humanity and a new humanity, or between
an apocalyptic darkness and an apocalyptic light. What, then,
could be a possible relationship between the anonymous
Jesus and the new anonymity that is being so forcefully
embodied in our midst? Surely we are being engulfed by a
new anonymity, one far more universal than anonymity has
ever been before, and one that could only be either an ending or a radical transformation of the self-consciousness
that we have known as the center of history, a self-

consciousness that is the very opposite of anonymity. Christianity inaugurated a full and actual self-consciousness that is a self-alienated and self-estranged consciousness, a divided and doubled consciousness that can know itself only by knowing its own intrinsic "other." That pure otherness is inseparable from the deeply interior "I," or inseparable from an interior "I" that is uniquely itself, but uniquely itself only by knowing itself as the very otherness of itself. Such an interior and intrinsic "other" was never manifest in the ancient world, just as an interior "subject" was never manifest or actual in that world. Only a deeply interior subject can know and realize radical otherness as its own, and this is the realization of the dichotomous center or subject of consciousness itself. That subject became the center of a uniquely Western self-consciousness, but it has nevertheless decisively been eroded under the impact of the modern realization of the death of God. Thence it has disappeared in our late modern imaginative and conceptual enactments, and is now becoming truly invisible in a new mass consciousness and society.

A new "electronic" humanity is now manifest as postmodernity, a humanity whose depth is indistinguishable from its surface or mask, and this is an anonymous humanity if only because it is a nameless humanity. Its actual name is everyone and no one at once, an everyone who can only be no one, but this is a no one who is the very opposite of a Buddhist selflessness. For it is a no one who is a wholly self-enclosed and passive desire, an anonymity without any possible integral or interior center, but nevertheless one consumed by a wholly impersonal and passive desire. Therewith, too, a new anonymity is also the very opposite of that self-consciousness from which postmodernity has evolved. Full self-consciousness could realize itself only by knowing its own center as the very opposite of itself, an otherness that is its own intrinsic "other." Such an essential and integral otherness is fully manifest in a uniquely modern soliloquy, and a uniquely modern self-portraiture as well, both of which are purely reversed in late modernity, a reversal inseparable from the deep dissolution of an actual self-consciousness. Is a new anonymous humanity a consequence of that dissolution? Does such an anonymity actualize itself by a dissolution of self-consciousness?

Certainly a new facelessness and voicelessness are the opposite of a unique and individual self-consciousness, and if the advent of a new and universal anonymity is the consequence of the dissolution of self-consciousness, then that anonymity is essentially related to self-consciousness. Only the negation of self-consciousness calls forth a universal anonymity, but that negation is a self-negation, a self-negation that is a final consequence of self-consciousness itself. A full and actual self-consciousness is historically unique, coming into existence only with the birth of Christianity, and perishing with the end of Christendom. That perishing, too, is historically unique, inseparable from that ultimate event which Nietzsche could proclaim as the death of God, but equally inseparable from what Hegel could essentially know as the full and final advent of Absolute Spirit. Hegel could know that advent as the end of art, an ending that is the ending of history itself, or at the very least the ending of our uniquely Western history, and therewith the ending of a uniquely Western self-consciousness. But that is a self-consciousness that was inaugurated by Christianity, and if the ending of self-consciousness impelled the advent of a new anonymous humanity, could the ending of the original Jesus have impelled the advent of self-consciousness itself?

Christianity knows self-consciousness as a dichotomous consciousness, one doubled and divided between freedom and impotence, wherein an individual freedom is enslaved by a universal movement of fall. This deep division and doubling of consciousness was discovered by Paul, and then realized internally and conceptually in Augustine's revolutionary theological thinking, which became the primary theological foundation of Western Christianity. The uniquely Western "subject," as established by this tradition, is not only in internal opposition to itself, but its own freedom is inseparable from the opposite of that freedom, an opposite that is not an external *ananke* or necessity but rather an internal necessity or destiny that is an internal enslavement and impotence. Augustine could discover his own individual freedom only by discovering the deep and internal impotence of his own uniquely individual will, a will that is the consequence of an original and universal fall. Yet that impotence or fallenness is the signature of our freedom, for its deepest source is finally ourselves. This realization embodies a new and radical freedom, a freedom that is a total responsibility, and even a responsibility for our own impotence. An Augustinian freedom of the will is precisely this responsibility, and just as it has been ever present in our deepest Western realizations of freedom, it is inseparable from a dark and internal ravaging guilt. This is the guilt that Christianity alone knows as a universal damnation, a damnation which is the necessary and inevitable consequence of a universal fall.

Consequently, in Western Christianity grace is inseparable from sin, or the actualization of grace is inseparable from a realization of sin, and the absolute grace that is the source of justification is inseparable from the realization of original sin. Justification, which is the sole source of an actual freedom for a fallen humanity, is realized only by grace, because of the absolute bondage of the fallen will. Yet justification occurs only once, in that once and for all event that Christianity knows as the crucifixion, a

crucifixion that is not only the death of the humanity of
Jesus, but a full and actual death of the Christ who is fully
human and fully divine at once. Thus the absolute grace of
the crucifixion is the death of the "I" of Jesus and the "I"
of God simultaneously, a death embodying an absolute
reversal that Christianity knows as resurrection, and hence
a reversal calling forth an absolutely new "I." Christian
Gnosticism knows the resurrected "I" as a purely primordial and purely spiritual "I," an "I" wholly free of any
possible division or doubling, hence a wholly unfallen "I."
Yet an incarnate or "worldly" Christianity realizes an
embodied "I" that is flesh and Spirit simultaneously, or sin
and grace at once, and therefore an "I" that is not only
deeply divided against itself, but that is itself its own opposite or "other." This is that internal opposition which
realizes the freedom of the will, a unique freedom inseparable from an all-consuming impotence, a self-division or
self-alienation that could only be a dichotomous division,
but thereby it is the center of self-consciousness itself.

Nevertheless, the center of self-consciousness is poten-
tially and implicitly a new anonymous consciousness. In
being deeply divided against itself, it can truly act only by
negating itself, thereby negating its own individual uniqueness, even if this negation is a fulfillment of itself. This is
precisely the negation that Hegels knows as a kenotic "self-
negation," or which Nietzsche calls forth as that absolute
act which is absolue No-saying and absolute Yes-saying at
once, or which Blake envisions as a universal "Self-
Annihilation." So it is that a uniquely Western and Christian freedom is inseparable from a uniquely Western and
Christian "bad conscience," just as a uniquely Western and
Christian ethical imperative is inseparable from a uniquely
Western and Christian repression. Such a pure negativity is
unique in world history, and if it becomes universal in the

historical world of late modernity, it has perhaps been transcended with the advent of postmodernity, but transcended
only as a consequence of its own consummation.

Nothing is more distinctive of our Western and Christian
tradition than its centering upon death and evil, a death
that is an eternal death and an evil that is an ultimate
nothingness. No such death and evil are present in Buddhism, or in any other non-Christian horizon, just as they
are absent from a once-born or "healthy-minded" Christianity. Already Augustine knew evil not simply as a privation
of being but as a real and actual nothingness, an understanding of evil absent in his Neoplatonic roots, just as it is
in the pre-Christian world as a whole. For Christianity could
know an ultimate redemption only by knowing an ultimate
judgment, or an eternal life that is inseparable from eternal
death. Even the unique individuality of a Christian self-
consciousness is inseparable from the anonymity of an ultimate nothingness of evil and death. Christianity has far
more deeply and far more comprehensively than any other
tradition enacted an eternal damnation and an eternal death.
But Christianity alone knows an absolute life that is realized only through an absolute death.

It is of ultimate importance that Gotama and Jesus are
unique among the prophets of the world in so centering
their call to liberation upon a calling forth of the way of
death. But whereas Gotama can unveil the bondage of the
human condition as an ultimate illusion unveiled in the
chain of causation or dependent origination, Jesus calls
forth an ultimate damnation and guilt that had been known
by no earlier prophet. Not only is damnation or ultimate
judgment continually called forth by Jesus, but damnation
and Hell dominate the New Testament as they do no other
scripture in the world. Here, simply to be awakened to the
ultimacy of the human condition is to know the eternal

judgment of damnation, a judgment that is all in all, or all in all to a fallen humanity, so that only a total reversal of that humanity can be a realization of grace. While that grace is the total grace of the Kingdom of God, its very advent is the ultimate and final reversal of the deepest darkness, and a darkness only manifest in that darkness itself.

Thus the actual name of Jesus calls forth a total grace that is inseparable from a total darkness, here an ultimate *coincidentia oppositorum* is fully manifest and real, a dialectical identity not only of an absolute life and an absolute death, but of a new apocalyptic humanity and a new apocalyptic desert and abyss. This is the abyss that is not only actualized in the crucifixion but is then reborn in a new self-consciousness that is absolutely polarized by its ultimately dichotomous ground. Nowhere in the world are true opposites so conjoined and united as they are in Christianity. No other tradition or way has known a redeemer and a redemption that inevitably call forth their opposites in Satan and Hell. And no other tradition had known an eternal life that is inseparable from an eternal death, or a Spirit that is not only actualized through body and flesh, but is the consequence of the epiphany or realization of Spirit itself in the deepest depths of matter and body. And if Western Christianity inaugurated a universal realization of freedom, here freedom has been inseparable from its opposite in predestination, for not even in Islam has predestination been so theologically overwhelming as it has been in Western Christianity, each of whose truly major theologians from Augustine and Aquinas through Luther, Calvin, and Barth, have been theologians of freedom only insofar as they have been theologians of predestination or election.

A ravaging dichotomy has dominated Christian history, and not only a dichotomy between the Kingdom of Christ and the Kingdom of Satan, but one between a new interior freedom and a new interior bondage and guilt, and between an absolutely sovereign and transcendent God and an absolutely compassionate and sacrificial Christ. But Christianity has embodied an evolutionary movement that is unique in history, one already present in the radical transformation of primitive Christianity into Catholic Christianity, then finally present in the end of Christendom itself, which ushered in the advent of a universal anonymity. Yet if the Christian can know Jesus as an apocalyptic humanity, then that humanity is inevitably anonymous, at least from the perspective of an old humanity. Inevitably, a genuinely universal consciousness is an anonymous consciousness. If it is actualized in the depths of self-consciousness, then its realization is necessarily a dichotomous realization. Therein anonymity and self-consciousness are inseparable from one another, or inseparable until each fully realizes itself. If this has occurred in the ending of the historical world of Christendom, that ending issues not only in a final advent of a universal humanity, but in a final ending of the interiority of self-consciousness itself. So that is an ending that is simultaneously a beginning, the beginning of a universal anonymity, or an anonymous consciousness that is quite simply consciousness itself.

Blake could speak for every Christian in calling forth Jesus as the "Universal Humanity" (*Jerusalem* 96:5), a universal body that is present in every human face and voice, and above all present in our deepest pain and joy. For the "I" that is the deepest center of suffering and joy is finally the "I" of Jesus. Accordingly, that center is both fully Jesus and fully anonymous at once, and is most fully Jesus by being most fully anonymous, an anonymity that is the anonymity of Jesus, even as its universality is the universality of Jesus. The "I" of Jesus is the incarnate "I," present in the depths of body or matter itself. But this incarnate "I" is the "I" of the Christ of passion and not the Christ of glory, the crucified and not the heavenly "I," or the "I" that is eternal death and eternal life at once. It is precisely eternal death that embodies a universal humanity, an embodiment freed from every primordial and transcendent ground, and just thereby an actually universal humanity. Yet the advent of a free and truly individual "I" is the consequence of the birth of a universal humanity. Only an embodied humanity could be a site for a fully actual self-consciousness. For only a fully and finally embodied humanity makes possible the inauguration of our interior depths, depths whose realization is impossible apart from the deepest incarnation of "I" or Spirit.

Nevertheless, these depths are deeply divided or doubled depths, divided between a new interior or within and a new body that is the body of these depths themselves. This is the new body that is the resurrected body, an apocalyptic resurrection occurring not in heaven but in a new aeon or new world. Gnosticism is a primary consequence of this resurrection, one fleeing or reversing an apocalyptic resurrection and creating an absolute dualism between the interior and the exterior or the within and the without. Such dualism is the very opposite of the dichotomous center of self-consciousness, a center whose opposites are wholly within, and even within the horizon of a new body or world. For the Christian world is the most dichotomous of all historical worlds, the one most deeply divided by opposing opposites, most deeply driven asunder by both external and internal forces. Here, these warring polarities are truly within, and not only interiorly within but historically within Christianity itself, a Christianity whose orthodoxy is not only inseparable from heresy, but whose center in Christ is the most dichotomous center in world history. So that if the

crucifixion is an ultimately and even absolutely dichotomous act, an act that is an absolute self-negation, self-
negation is the center of Christian history even as it is the
center of a uniquely Christian consciousness.

Self-negation is actualized in our deepest interior movements, movements realizing the dichotomous center of
self-consciousness, apart from which a full and genuine
self-consciousness is unreal. True self-consciousness is
inevitably a negative consciousness, most deeply assaulting
and negating itself, so that the actuality of self-consciousness
is inseparable from the actuality of self-alienation and self-
laceration. Apart from such deep and interior negativity
self-consciousness is hollow and unreal, and nowhere more
unreal than in what presents itself as self-consciousness
today. This is ever more fully manifest as a simulated
consciousness, a simulation that is not only an electronic
simulation, but one manifest wherever contemporary consciousness is open and real, or wherever consciousness is
truly actual in our world. Such a simulated consciousness
is inevitably anonymous, yet this new anonymity is at
once both truly anonymous and truly universal. Now anonymity is universal as it has never been before, but this is
a new universality embodying the end of self-consciousness, or the ending of the very center of self-consciousness. For that ending issues in a truly new anonymity only
made possible by the absence of all genuine interiority, an
absence that is the actual ending of any possible center or
subject of interiority itself. Consequently, the universal
presence we know is inseparable and indistinguishable from
a universal absence, a universal absence of an actual interiority, and therefore a universal absence of the unique and
individual "I."

A universal absence is a truly new absence, historically
unique. A new anonymity is also and even thereby a new

ahistorical consciousness, one that consumes its history
by forgetting it, and unlike all previous forgetting, it occurs not only in the context of preserving vast quantities
of historical data, but also in the context of transforming
all past historical time into a purely and totally ahistorical
present. Thereby a truly new simultaneity of time has been
born, a unique simultaneity of historical time. Here, not
only do a historical past and a historical present coincide,
but past, present, and future are all simultaneous, because
no time whatsoever can stand outside of such a total presence. Unlike a primordial simultaneity, or a mystical simultaneity, this is a simultaneity in which time itself is a
wholly abstract or simulated time, and most abstract to
the extent that it is simultaneous. So likewise are we being
overwhelmed by a new ubiquity of space, a space that is
omnidirectional, without any actual direction or perspective. Thereby center as center has truly disappeared, just
as circumference as circumference has disappeared. Already
in the twelfth century, Alan of Lille could formulate a new
Neoplatonic maxim: "God is an intelligible sphere, whose
center is everywhere and the circumference nowhere." But
with the modern realization of the death of God, it is a
new infinite space whose center is everywhere and whose
circumference is nowhere, a space both macroscopic and
microscopic, and a new ubiquity of space inseparable from
a new simultaneity of time. That time and space can only
be wholly abstract and wholly simulated for us, unless at
bottom we truly are a new radical anonymity, and an apocalyptic anonymity now becoming all in all.

Can we truly know Jesus as such a radical anonymity?
Ironically, both Blake and Hegel could know the dead body
of Jesus as such an anonymity, a body that is resurrected
as the "Lord of glory," but resurrected only insofar as it
ceases to be body or earth. Such resurrection is ascension,

and not the ascension of an earthly body, but only the
ascension of a glorified and heavenly body. This is just the
spiritual body that Gnosticism knows as Jesus, a body that
is the dualistic and not dialectical "other" of the earthly
body, an earthly body here known as an alien abyss. Blake
and every radical Christian seer can name the Gnostic
Christ or Heaven as an all-too-human Hell, just as Blake
could know the Christ of glory as a vision of Satan, a Satan
who is the deepest ground of alienation and repression,
and whose alienated body is an absolutely repressed energy and life. Is that Ulro which Blake knew as the body
of Satan only now being fully born? Or are we being confronted by that Jerusalem who is the *coincidentia
oppositorum* of Christ and Satan, of Heaven and Hell? If
the Christian knows an absolutely alienated and repressed
body as the body of Satan, does the Christian know the
incarnation of Christ as an incarnation in that body, and
thus know the contemporary Jesus as a real and actual
emptiness?

Now an actual emptiness is not a primordial emptiness,
not the emptiness of nirvana, but rather an emptiness that
is *here* and *now* and nowhere else. Indeed, an actual anonymity is nowhere else but *here* and *now*. So it is not the
anonymity of the Buddha, but rather the anonymity of an
everybody who is nobody, or of an everyone who is no one.
If that "no one" is an apocalyptic and not a primordial
"nobody," an anonymity that is the consummation of history itself, then it is the consummation of a real and actual history. While such a consummation is the end of
history, this is an ending that precisely thereby is truly
ending, hence an apocalyptic ending. Our most prophetic
Christians have invariably known the ending of history as
occurring in their own time, and thus have inevitably
known the apocalyptic Jesus, an apocalyptic Jesus who is

the totality of Christ. But only in our time is an apocalyptic Jesus a fully anonymous Jesus, or a universal Jesus who is "nobody." Is that "nobody" finally a tomb, a tomb veiling the dead body it encloses, so that a new universal Jesus is at bottom a renewal of the dead body in the sepulchre? Christianity can know that body as making possible a descent into Hell that alone can mediate redemption to the dead, so that if our new humanity is a new body of death and nothingness, perhaps only a renewal of the descent into Hell can make redemption possible today. Certainly the imagination of late modernity has again and again enacted a descent into Hell. Even if this is a descent with no possibility of resurrection, or no possibility of a heavenly resurrection, it is all too realistic precisely because of that, and most realistic in its very movement of descent.

Indeed, it is the heavenly Jesus or the Christ of glory who is most distant from us. Thus if the way "up" for us is inevitably the way "down," then we can know only a Jesus who has descended into Hell, and not a Jesus who has ascended into Heaven. To know another Jesus would be to know a Jesus who has no actual point of contact with us, yet to know a Jesus who has descended into Hell would be to know a Jesus who is incarnate for us. If a totally incarnate Jesus is a totally descended Jesus, then a new anonymity could be a new body of Jesus, and even if that body is a body of death, it is a body making possible a mediation of redemption to the dead. The public or manifest expressions of a uniquely modern Christianity have refused the descent into Hell, despite the fact that our deepest modern seers have repeatedly envisioned a descent into Hell, and even envisioned it as an apocalyptic and final descent. This is the descent embodying the deepest ending, and one calling forth a truly new and universal anonymity. Such anonymity is certainly apocalyptic, possible only as a consequence of an apocalyptic ending, and embodied only in the realm of the dead. Yet this is a truly new kingdom of death, and absolutely new if only because of its comprehensive universality. Apocalypticism has always known a resurrection of the dead, but a new and contemporary apocalypticism knows a resurrection that is the inauguration of Hell and of Hell alone, thus reversing the ancient hope in resurrection.

If the uniquely modern realization of the death of God is simultaneously the death or ending of a uniquely individual self-consciousness, then the ending of the "I" of God and the ending of our deeply interior "I" are one event. As Kierkegaard knew so deeply, this ushers in a total objectification of consciousness and society, one negating all interior and individual subjectivity. Hence the death of God is the advent of our new anonymity, an apocalyptic event repeating and renewing an original Christian apocalypticism, but now an apocalyptic totality is a pure and total anonymity. Christianity knows the crucifixion as the one absolutely apocalyptic event that has already occurred, and if that event is repeated and renewed in the modern realization of the death of God, such an apocalyptic repetition can be known as the actualization of the death of God in the fullness of time and space itself. Now crucifixion is all in all, even as the death of God is all in all, but now an all in all grounded in a kingdom of emptiness and death.

Even if such emptiness is publicly invisible because it is so fully disguised, it is dislodged in our deepest moments that occur not only in our deeper imaginative and conceptual acts, but also in our rare moments of silence and solitude. Then we become aware of that new death that is engulfing us, and while the deepest religious moments have inevitably been moments of death, these once brought a joy that is now wholly absent, and nothing so characterizes our world as does the deep absence of joy. Kierkegaard could know contemporaneity with Christ as the deepest movement of faith, a contemporaneity that is a repetition of the absolute death of the crucifixion, and thereby a repetition of the descent into Hell. Such a contemporaneity is present in every truly kenotic or self-emptying Christianity, or in every repetition and renewal of the crucifixion. But if our world is a universally empty world, a truly universal and actual emptiness that is unique in history, then our world could be an embodiment of the Jesus who has descended into Hell, an embodiment of that ultimate and final abyss actualized by the crucifixion. That abyss is a total abyss, a total nothingness, but a total nothingness that here alone is actuality itself.

Yet this abyss of total nothingness is released by a total self-negation or self-emptying. Our prophetic forbears from Paul and Augustine through Eckhart, Blake, and Joyce have known the depths of self-negation as a self-annihilation of the deepest depths of the "I," depths only called forth by this self-negation, and depths finally comprehending both the "I" of humanity and the "I" of God at once. Is that "I" finally a totally anonymous "I," a pure nothingness, and yet a purely actual and totally present nothingness? The Christian epic tradition from Dante through Joyce evolves from the pure nothingness of Hell only to culminate in the pure nothingness of a uniquely Christian Heaven, a Heaven not only inseparable but indistinguishable from Hell, or a redemption indistinguishable from damnation. This tradition finally and ultimately celebrates a Christ who is indistinguishable from Satan, one implicitly present in Milton and explicitly present in Blake and Joyce, and a Christ who is perhaps present today in a totally anonymous and empty humanity.

Nothing is more uniquely his own than is the death of Jesus, a death repeated and renewed in every kenotic actualization, actualizations that have inevitably called forth truly new worlds. Could such a new world be present in our midst? And present in its apparent absence, an absence of everything which we can know as grace or life, or of anything or anyone who could openly or manifestly be present as Jesus? Certainly an anonymous Jesus could bear no marks or signs of anyone whom we once knew as Jesus, unless the kenotic actuality of Jesus fulfills itself in a full negation of those signs, a negation issuing not only in an absolutely anonymous body or "I," but in an actuality that is a full and final embodiment of self-negation or self-annihilation. Such an actuality could not be a primordial emptiness or nothingness, not a nothingness that is an original pleroma. For in being an actual emptiness or nothingness it could only be an immediate actuality, one fully and purely actual in its own realization or actualization of itself. And unlike any possible primordial pleroma, or any possible original emptiness, such an actuality would inevitably be inseparable from its own polar "other." Only thereby could it be an immediate actuality, an immediacy impossible apart from the pure "otherness" of its ground, an otherness alone making possible immediacy itself. Such an immediacy is wholly absent in a pure innocence, being present only in what Blake called forth as "experience," or in what Nietzsche celebrated as "body" and earth. An immediate actuality can be present only by way of the horizon of its own essential and intrinsic "other," an "other" manifest and real today in a wholly passive impassivity, or in a new and ultimate immobility and bondage, or in a truly hollow and artificial "I." If such an "I" is finally quite simply nothing, it would thereby be the intrinsic opposite of a purely kenotic actuality of pure self-negation or self-emptying, a self-negation that is finally and ultimately reality itself.

No doubt an absolute self-emptying can publicly and commonly by manifest as a literal emptiness or nothingness, and an absolute self-annihilation can commonly be seen and known as being quite simply and only a suicidal death. So likewise a pure passivity can publicly be manifest as a pure desire, a simply empty and immobile "I" can present itself as a pure "I," a truly frozen and impotent body can be masked as a body of passion, and a dying and wholly self-enclosed humanity can commonly appear as a vibrantly living humanity. All of these illusions are intrinsic to our anonymous state and condition, but they parallel illusions of a far deeper kind, those veiling our ultimate condition and situation. While these are unveiled in our deepest vision, they are not unveiled apart from the ultimacy of death and nothingness, or apart from an absolute judgment that Christianity knows as damnation. So it is that a Christian resurrection is vacuous and unreal apart from the crucifixion, even as life itself is unreal apart from death, and an absolute life wholly unreal apart from an absolute death.

The Christian symbol of the crucifixion is clearly a calling forth of an absolute death that is an absolute compassion, here compassion and death are not only inseparable but indistinguishable, and if no other symbol is more uniquely Christian, paradoxically and perhaps not so paradoxically no other true symbol is so powerful in our world. Would it be possible to name a truly major work of the late modern imagination that is not grounded in what at the very least is a reverse or inverted repetition of the crucifixion? Although such works are commonly veiled or elusive, and most so the musical and visual expressions of our imagination, when they are linguistically open and clear, as in our deepest poetry, drama, and prose, a deep self-negation is clearly manifest, and one occurring in an ultimate abyss and darkness. This is an abyss that Christianity knows as being realized only in the crucifixion, this abyss and this abyss alone here realizes redemption, hence it has an ultimacy that is present nowhere else, one inducing an ultimate and even absolute response.

Only the crucifixion could be a total symbol in authentic Christianity, one apart from which the love of God can only be known as absolute judgment, and the creation only finally manifest as an abysmal nothingness. The Christian knows the crucifixion alone as embodying an absolute compassion, a compassion that Jesus could name and enact as the dawning of the Kingdom of God. That kingdom is certainly not a sovereign, majestic, and heavenly kingdom, otherwise it could not possibly be embodied in the crucifixion, or could not possibly be a kenotic or self-emptying totality. Jesus is the Christian name of that self-emptying, and if Jesus has become a wholly anonymous Jesus for us, that self-emptying could only be a wholly anonymous actuality for us, and most anonymous in its actual presence as self-emptying. Yet an actual presence is an immediate presence, and one therefore inseparable from its own inherent "other," and if never before has Jesus been so invisible and unheard, that could be a decisive sign of his total presence. So it is that the abstract and simulated world of our anonymity would appear to be the very opposite of the kenotic actuality of self-emptying, but just thereby it might well be the only possible horizon for the realization of a wholly anonymous Jesus.

If only in its totality, or its dawning totality, the very uniqueness of our world is inseparable from a dissolution or erasure of all interior uniqueness. There is now far more objective knowledge and objective actuality than ever before, but a subjective interiority has never been so precarious, just as a genuinely human future has never been so totally in question. Yes, a new total presence is dawning in our midst, but it is a total absence of everything we once knew as either world or humanity. Ours is surely a truly apocalyptic situation, the most apocalyptic situation in our history, one transcending even an original Christian apocalypticism in the totality of its historical enactment. All past historical worlds are now being dissolved, and even all truly natural and sacred realms as well. Yet could such a dissolution be in genuine continuity with an original apocalypticism? Could our contemporary dissolution ultimately be a kenotic and self-emptying dissolution? A silent horror and abyss that is finally a divine abyss, the abyss of the crucifixion itself? And a divine abyss that is cosmic and historical at once, interior and exterior at once, thereby embodying an anonymity of Jesus that is an abysmal but nevertheless a truly universal anonymity? A truly universal body and world that is precisely thereby a total *coincidentia oppositorum* of Satan and Christ?

NOTES

Prologue

1. Karl Barth, *The Epistle to the Romans,* trans. Edwyn C. Hoskins (London: Oxford University Press, 1933), p. 98.

2. Georg Wilhelm Friedrich Hegel, *Lectures on the Philosophy of Religion,* ed. Peter C. Hodgson (Berkeley: University of California Press, 1988), pp. 463–65.

3. Augustine, *De Trinitate* 1:28 and 4:6.

4. Aquinas, *Summa Theologica* 3:50.

5. Karl Barth, *Church Dogmatics,* vol. 2.

6. Hans Urs von Balthasar, *Mysterious Paschale: The Mystery of Easter,* trans. Aidan Nichols (Grand Rapids, Mich.: Eerdmans, 1990).

7. Søren Kierkegaard, *Philosophical Fragments.*

Chapter One. The Apocalyptic Jesus

1. Cf. John P. Meier, *A Marginal Jew: Rethinking the Historical Jesus* (New York: Anchor Bible Reference Library/ Doubleday, 1994), 2:237–72.

2. Rudolf Bultmann, *Theology of the New Testament,* trans. Kendrick Grobel (New York: Scribner's, 1955), 2:63.

3. *Ibid.,* p. 66.

4. Albert Schweitzer, *In Quest of the Historical Jesus: A Critical Study of Its Progress from Reimarus to Wrede,* trans. W. Montgomery (London: Adam & Charles Black, 1954), p. 401.

Chapter Two. The Jesus Seminar

1. *The Five Gospels: The Search for the Authentic Words of Jesus,* New Testament translation and commentary by Robert

W. Funk, Roy W. Hoover, and the Jesus Seminar (New York, Macmillan, 1993).

2. Rudolf Otto, *The Kingdom of God and the Son of Man,* trans. Floyd V. Filson and Bertram Lee-Woolf (London: Lutterworth Press, 1943), pp. 72, 146–47.

3. G. W. F. Hegel, *Three Essays, 1793–1795,* ed. and trans. Peter Fuss and John Dobbins (Notre Dame, Ind.: University of Notre Dame Press, 1984), pp. 104–65.

Chapter Three. Crossan's Jesus

1. John Dominic Crossan, *The Historical Jesus: The Life of a Mediterranean Jewish Peasant* (San Francisco: Harper, 1991).

2. See Crossan's article in *Jesus and Faith,* ed. Jeffrey Carlson and Robert A. Ludwig (Maryknoll, N.Y.: Orbis Books, 1994), p. 150.

3. Ibid., p. 163.

4. Crossan, *The Historical Jesus,* p. 332.

5. *Jesus and Faith,* p. 5.

6. John Dominic Crossan, *Finding Is the First Act: Trove Folktales and Jesus' Treasure Parable* (Fortress Press/Scholars Press, 1979).

7. *Ibid.,* p. 94.

8. John Dominic Crossan, *Cliffs of Fall: Paradox and Polyvalence in the Parables of Jesus* (New York: Seabury Press, 1980).

9. Max Weber, *Ancient Judaism,* trans. and ed. Hans H. Gerth and Don Martindale (Free Press, 1952), pp. 278–80.

10. *Jesus and Faith,* p. 153.

11. Norman K. Gottwald, *The Tribes of Yahweh: A Sociology of the Religion of Liberated Israel, 1250–1050 B.C.E.* (Maryknoll: Orbis Books, 1979).

12. *The Harper Atlas of the Bible,* ed. James B. Pritchard (New York: Harper & Row, 1987), pp. 62–63.

Chapter Four. The Gnostic Jesus

1. *The Origins of Gnosticism: Colloquium of Messiana* (Leiden: E. J. Brill, 1967), p. xxvii.

2. James M. Robinson, "On Bridging the Gulf: From Q to the Gospel of Thomas (or Vice Versa)," in *Nag Hammadi, Gnosticism, and Early Christianity,* ed. Charles W. Hedrick and Robert Hodgson, Jr. (Peabody, Mass.: Hendrickson, 1986), pp. 128–35.

3. Robert McLachlan Wilson, "Gnosis, Gnosticism, and the New Testament," in *The Origins of Gnosticism,* p. 525.

4. Hans Jonas, *Gnosis,* 1:214–15. Quoted in Kurt Rudolph, *Gnosis: The Nature and History of Gnosticism,* trans. and ed. Robert McLachlan Wilson (San Francisco: Harper & Row, 1983), p. 265.

5. Hans Jonas, *The Gnostic Religion: The Message of the Alien God and the Beginnings of Christianity* (Boston: Beacon Press, 1958), p. 237.

6. Hans Jonas, "Delimitation of the Gnostic Phenomenon— Typological and Historical," in *The Origins of Gnosticism,* p. 92.

7. *Ibid.,* p. 95.

8. *Ibid.,* p. 106.

9. Helmut Koester, *Ancient Christian Gospels: Their History and Development* (Philadelphia: Trinity Press International, 1990).

10. *The Gnostic Scriptures,* trans. and intro. Bentley Layton (New York: Doubleday, 1987), p. 254.

11. *Ibid.,* p. 255.

12. *Ibid.,* p. 322.

13. *Ibid.,* p. 239.

14. *Ibid.,* p. 297.

15. *Ibid.,* p. 250.

16. *Ibid.,* p. 37.

17. *The Anchor Bible: The Epistles of John,* trans. and intro. Raymond E. Brown (New York: Doubleday, 1982), pp. 685–93.

18. Cf. Martin Werner, *The Formation of Christian Dogma: An Historical Study of its Problem,* trans. S. G. F. Brandon (London: Adam & Charles Black, 1957).

19. *Ibid.,* p. 196.

20. St. Thomas Aquinas, *Summa Theologica,* trans. Fathers of the English Dominican Province (New York: Benziger Brothers), 2:2034.

21. *Ibid.,* p. 2272.

208

NOTES

22. *Ibid.*, p. 2057.
23. *Ibid.*, p. 2040.

Chapter Five. The Pauline Jesus

1. Introduction to James M. Robinson and Helmut Koester's *Trajectories through Early Christianity* (Philadelphia: Fortress Press, 1971), p. 10.
2. Rudolf Bultmann, *Theology of the New Testament,* trans. Kendrick Grobel (New York: Scribner's, 1951), 1:188.
3. Elaine Hiesey Pagels, *The Gnostic Paul: Gnostic Exegesis of the Pauline Letters* (Philadelphia: Fortress Press, 1975).
4. *Ibid.*, p. 76.
5. *Ibid.*, p. 135.
6. *Ibid.*, p. 137.
7. Albert Schweitzer, *The Mysticism of Paul the Apostle,* trans. William Montgomery (London: Adam & Charles Black, 1931).
8. Rudolf Bultmann, *The Second Letter to the Corinthians,* ed. Erich Dinkler, trans. Roy A. Harrisville (Minneapolis: Augsburg, 1985), pp. 164–75.
9. Ernst Kaesemann, *Commentary on Romans,* trans. and ed. Geoffrey W. Bromiley (Grand Rapids, Mich.: Eerdmans, 1980).
10. J. Christiaan Beker, *Paul the Apostle: The Triumph of God in Life and Thought* (Philadelphia: Fortress Press, 1980).

Chapter Six. The Catholic Jesus

1. Michael O'Carroll, C.S.Sp., *Theotokos: A Theological Encyclopedia of the Blessed Virgin May* (Collegeville, Minn.: Liturgical Press, 1982), p. 112.
2. J. Glen Taylor, "Was Yahweh Worshipped as the Sun?" *Biblical Archaeology Review* (May/June 1994): 90.
3. Cf. Hans Conzelmann, "The Mother of Wisdom," in *The Future of Our Religious Past: Essays in Honour of Rudolf Bultmann,* ed. James M. Robinson, trans. Charles E. Carlston

and Robert P. Scharlemann (New York: Harper & Row, 1971), pp. 230–43.

4. Layton, *The Gnostic Scriptures*, p. 233.

5. *Ibid.*, p. 298.

6. *Ibid.*, p. 80.

7. O'Carroll, *Theotokos*, p. 189.

8. *Ibid.*, p. 138.

9. *Ibid.*, p. 160.

10. *Ibid.*, p. 163.

11. *Ibid.*, p. 2.

12. Cf. Thomas J. J. Altizer, "The Birth of Vision," *History as Apocalypse* (Albany: State University of New York Press, 1985), pp. 17–29.

13. Dante Alighieri, *The Divine Comedy: Paradiso* [Bollingen Series No. 80], trans. Charles S. Singleton (Princeton, N.J.: Princeton University Press, 1975), p. 371.

14. James Joyce, *Ulysses* (New York: Modern Library, 1934), p. 207. Unfortunately it is still necessary to employ this edition of *Ulysses*, if only because its "corrected text," as edited by Hans Walter Gabler (New York: Random House, 1986), has proven to be so controversial.

15. Stanislaus Joyce, *My Brother's Keeper: James Joyce's Early Years* (New York: Viking, 1958), p. 105.

16. The deepest calling forth of a contemporary Catholic and apocalyptic transformation of the *missa solemnis* into the *missa jubilaea* occurs in D. G. Leahy, *Novitas Mundi: Perceptions of the History of Being* (Albany: State University of New York Press, 1994), pp. 344–96. Cf. Thomas J. J. Altizer, "The Contemporary Challenge of Radical Catholicism," *Journal of Religion* (April 1994): 182–98.

Chapter Seven. The Protestant Jesus

1. Heiko A. Oberman, *The Dawn of the Reformation: Essays in Late Medieval and Early Reformation Thought* (Grand Rapids, Mich.: Eerdmans, 1992), p. 2.

2. Heiko A. Oberman, *Luther: Man between God and the Devil*, trans. Eileen Walliser-Schwarzbart (New York: Doubleday, 1992), p. 104.

3. Martin Luther, *Lectures on Romans*, trans. and ed. Wilhelm Pauck (Philadelphia: Westminster Press, 1961), p. 263.

4. *Complete Prose Works of John Milton. vol. 6: Christian Doctrine*, ed. Maurice Kelley, trans. John Carey (New Haven: Yale University Press, 1973), p. 204–12.

5. *Ibid.*, p. 275.

6. *Ibid.*, p. 303.

7. *Ibid.*, p. 310.

8. *Ibid.*, pp. 438–44.

9. *Ibid.*, p. 591.

10. *Ibid.*, p. 587.

11. *Ibid.*, pp. 521–31.

12. John Milton, *Paradise Lost and Paradise Regained*, ed. Christopher Ricks (New York: New American Library, 1968). All quotations are from this edition.

13. Milton, *Complete Prose Works*, 6:495–97.

14. Milton O. Percival, *William Blake's Circle of Destiny* (New York: Columbia University Press, 1938), p. 29.

Chapter Eight. The Nihilistic Jesus

1. *Selected Letters of Friedrich Nietzsche*, ed. and trans. Christopher Middleton (Chicago: University of Chicago Press, 1969), p. 327.

2. Joseph Frank, *Dostoevsky: The Stir of Liberation, 1860–1865* (Princeton, N.J.: Princeton University Press, 1986), pp. 167–72.

3. *Selected Letters of Fyodor Dostoyevsky*, ed. Joseph Frank and David L. Goldstein, trans. Andrew R. Macandrew (New Brunswick, N.J.: Rutgers University Press, 1987), pp. 331–32.

4. Fyodor Dostoevsky, *The Notebooks for the Possessed*, ed. Edward Wasiolek (Chicago: University of Chicago Press, 1969), p. 53.

5. *Ibid.*, p. 408.

6. Joseph Frank, *Dostoevsky: The Seeds of Revolt, 1821–1849* (Princeton, N.J.: Princeton University Press, 1976), p. 360.

7. Frank, *Dostoevsky: The Stir of Liberation*, p. 309.

8. Fyodor Dostoevsky, *Demons*, trans. Richard Pevear and Larissa Volokhonsky (New York: Alfred A. Knopf, 1994), p. 115. All quotations from *Demons* are from this translation.

9. Friedrich Nietzsche, *The Will to Power*, trans. Walter Kaufmann and R. J. Hollingdale (New York: Random House, 1967), p. 3.

10. Friedrich Nietzsche, *The Antichrist* 43, in *The Portable Nietzsche*, ed. trans. Walter Kaufmann (New York: Viking Press, 1954), p. 618. Subsequent quotations from *The Antichrist* are from this edition.

11. Nietzsche, *The Antichrist* 36, p. 609.

12. Nietzsche, *The Will to Power* 219, p. 128.

13. Nietzsche, *The Gay Science* 125, in *The Portable Nietzsche*, p. 95.

14. Nietzsche, *The Antichrist* 32, p. 606.

Chapter Nine. The Buddhist Jesus

1. Nishida Kitaro, *Last Writings: Nothingness and the Religious Worldview*, trans. and intro. David A. Dilworth (Honolulu: University of Hawaii Press, 1987), pp. 75–95.

2. Augustine, *The Trinity*, trans. Edmund Hill, O.P., ed. John E. Rotelle, O.S.A. (Brooklyn: New City Press, 1991), p. 86.

3. Augustine, *The Trinity* 1:3.

4. *Ibid.*, 4:6.

5. Karl Barth, *Church Dogmatics. Vol. 2: The Doctrine of God*, ed. G. W. Bromiley and T. F. Torrance (Edinburgh: T & T Clark, 1957), pp. 161–74, 340–54.

6. This chapter is the consequence of over forty years of work on the relationship between Christianity and Buddhism. The stages of my work are expressed in the following of my publications: "Religion and Reality," *Journal of Religion* 38 (October 1958): 171–83; *Oriental Mysticism and Biblical Eschatology*

(Philadelphia: Westminster Press, 1961), pp. 113–99; "Nirvana and Kingdom of God," *Journal of Religion* 43 (April 1963): 105–17; *The Gospel of Christian Atheism* (Philadelphia: Westminster Press, 1966), pp. 31–54; *The New Apocalypse: The Radical Christian Vision of William Blake* (East Lansing: Michigan State University Press, 1967), pp. 179–92; *The Descent into Hell* (Philadelphia: Lippincott, 1970), pp. 173–214; *The Self Embodiment of God* (New York: Harper & Row, 1977), pp. 8–26, 81–96; "An Inquiry into the Meaning of Negation in the Dialectical Logics of East and West," in *Religious Language and Knowledge,* ed. Robert H. Ayers and William T. Blackstone (Athens: University of Georgia Press, 1972), pp. 76–96; "Nirvana as a Negative Image of God," in *Buddhist and Western Philosophy,* ed. Nathan Katz (New Delhi: Sterling, 1981), pp. 18–29; "Buddhist Emptiness and the Crucifixion of God," in *The Emptying God: A Buddhist-Christian-Jewish Conversation,* ed. John B. Cobb, Jr., and Christopher Ives (Maryknoll, N.Y.: Orbis Books, 1990), pp. 69–78; "Emptiness and God," in *The Religious Philosophy of Nishitani Keiji,* ed. Taitetsu Unno (Berkeley: Asian Humanities Press, 1989), pp. 70–81; *Genesis and Apocalypse* (Louisville, Ky.: Westminster/John Knox Press, 1990), pp. 93–106; *The Genesis of God* (Louisville, Ky.: Westminster/John Knox Press, 1993), pp. 178–84.

V

Vajrayana Buddhism, 162
Vala (Blake), 129
Valentinian Gnosticism, 54, 57,
   59, 73–75, 85
Valentinus, 54–59, 91
Verkovensky, Pyotyr, 143,
   151–152
Virgil, 95, 99
voice, 20, 102
void, x, 17, 104

W

Weber, Max, 44
Weiss, Johannes, 72
Western Christianity, xiii, 158, 192
   consciousness, 9

"Wheel of Religion," 136
Wilder, Amos N., xi
will, 189–190, 193
will to nothingness, 29, 154
Will to Power, 143, 152, 158–159
Will to Power (Nietzsche), 152
Wisdom. *See* Sophia
wisdom tradition, 4, 10, 36, 39,
   48, 52–54, 86
Word of God, 5, 38, 72
world, xv, xviii–xix, xviii, 5,
   10–11, 14, 32, 34

Y

Yahweh, 6, 44–46, 90
Yes-saying, 13, 29, 155, 190
Yggdrasil, 109